BION AND BEING

BION AND BEING

Passion and the Creative Mind

Annie Reiner

Routledge
Taylor & Francis Group

LONDON AND NEW YORK

First published 2012 by Karnac Books Ltd.

Published 2019 by Routledge
2 Park Square, Milton Park, Abingdon, Oxon OX14 4RN
52 Vanderbilt Avenue, New York, NY 10017

Routledge is an imprint of the Taylor & Francis Group, an informa business

British Library Cataloguing in Publication Data

A C.I.P. for this book is available from the British Library

ISBN 978-1-85575-854-4 (pbk)

Edited, designed and produced by The Studio Publishing Services Ltd
www.publishingservicesuk.co.uk
e-mail: studio@publishingservicesuk.co.uk

CONTENTS

ACKNOWLEDGEMENTS

It is with great pleasure that I thank Barry Lebost for his scientific guidance and his profound metaphysical understanding. I am very grateful to Dr James Grotstein for his always erudite thoughts about the manuscript. Special thanks also to Dr Susan Williams and Mrs Susan Grotstein for their support and careful reading of the book, and to Jenny Okun and Jorge Davies for their artistic talents, friendship, and generosity. Last, I thank my father, who sometimes claims not to understand what I am writing about, but whose capacity for contact with "O" is an inspiration.

Permissions

I am grateful for permission to use material from the following works:

From "a total stranger one black day". Copyright © 1957, 1985, 1991 by the Trustees for the E. E. Cummings Trust, from *Complete Poems: 1904{-}1962* by E. E. Cummings, edited by George J. Firmage. Used by permission of Liveright Publishing Corporation.

Dickinson, E. (1959). *Selected Poems and Letters of Emily Dickinson*, Anchor Doubleday Press: New York. Reprinted with the permission of the Estate of Robert N. Linscott.

Jean, M. (Ed.) (1974). *Jean Arp, Collected French Writings*. London: Calder & Boyars. The translation is reproduced by permission of Oneworld Classics: Surrey, UK. From *Jours Éffeuillés* by Jean Arp © Éditions Gallimard, Paris, 1966.

Kees Bolle, *The Bhagavadgita: A New Translation*. © 1979 by the Regents of the University of California. Published by the University of California Press.

Pablo Neruda, excerpt from poem "LIX," El Libro De Las Preguntas © Fundación Pablo Neruda, 2011.

Pablo Neruda, excerpt from LIX, translated by William O'Daly, from *The Book of Questions*. Copyright © 1974 by Pablo Neruda and the Heirs of Pablo Neruda. Translation copyright © 1991, 2001 by William O'Daly. Reprinted with the permission of The Permissions Company, Inc., on behalf of Copper Canyon Press, www.coppercanyonpress.org

From Duino Elegies by Rainer Maria Rilke, translated by David Young. Copyright © 1978 by W. W. Norton & Company, Inc. Used by permission of W. W. Norton & Company, Inc.

From *Love is a Stranger: Selected Lyric Poetry of Jelaluddin Rumi*, Translated by Kabir Edmund Helminski, Originally published by Threshold Books, 1993.

From *Magnificent One*. Trans. Ergin, N. by Rumi. Original publisher: Larson Publications, NY, 1993. Reprinted with the permission of Nevit Oguz Ergin.

ABOUT THE AUTHOR

Annie Reiner, PhD, PsyD, LCSW, is a member and senior faculty member of The Psychoanalytic Center of California (PCC) in Los Angeles, and a fellow of the International Psychoanalytical Association (IPA). Her work was influenced by the ideas of Wilfred Bion, with whom she studied briefly in the 1970s. Her psychoanalytic writings have been published in many journals and anthologies, and her previous book, *The Quest For Conscience and The Birth of the Mind*, was published by Karnac (2009). In addition to her psychoanalytic work, Dr Reiner is a poet, playwright, and author–illustrator of children's books. She maintains a private practice in Beverly Hills, California.

Introduction

Bion introduced a new psychoanalytic space in which to explore the mind. This new space is reflected in his concept of O, in my view the background to all of his work, which therefore forms a large part of the focus of this book. By now, his ideas are widely known throughout the analytic world, and yet the revolutionary meaning of some of these ideas has, in certain ways, been underestimated. This is especially true of his concept of O, which has brought to psychoanalysis the metaphysical perspective of the mystic. It represents a global change that affects all aspects of analytic work, for it shifts our perspective of the kind of mind necessary to conduct an analysis. It is this change that I will examine.

Grotstein makes this statement, *à propos* of the dramatic consequences of this idea:

> I believe that the concept of O transforms all existing psychoanalytic theories (e.g. the pleasure principle, the death instinct, and the paranoid–schizoid and depressive positions) into veritable psychoanalytic manic defenses against the unknown, unknowable, ineffable, inscrutable, ontological experience of ultimate being . . . (Grotstein, 2007, p. 121)

The concept of O represents a different psychical point of view, and all of our previous observations about the human mind are affected by this shift.

Bion's ideas have often been subject to confusion or misunderstanding, partially related to the fact that "O" represents an ineffable metaphysical state beyond rational understanding and, therefore, beyond verbal description. While Bion's influence is widespread, he seemed to be aware of the dangerous possibility of a person's being "loaded with honours [till he sinks] without a trace" (Bion, 1970, p. 78). Although this has not happened to him, Bion's ideas reflect complex realities, and efforts to simplify them or "understand" them intellectually have, at times, drained them of their essential mystery. Bion distrusted the very function of understanding as a limitation to one's ability to experience the non-sensual metaphysical mind, that is, to one's capacity for contact with O.

I have often been impressed by both the widespread dissemination and profound interest in Bion's work, as well as the confusion, particularly around this concept of O. Lively discussions have convinced me both of the enduring curiosity about this idea and the fear of the *emotional experience* it engenders. Then again, this kind of ambivalent feeling is always present in relation to these unknown and unknowable states of mind. Because of the difficulties in communicating about such ineffable states, I will make use of other metaphorical means in an effort to evoke something of their mystery through comparisons with artistic, scientific, religious, and philosophical truths. The works of creative artists who access this experience in their work will, I hope, help to provide emotional overtones to the theories of Bion and other psychoanalytic thinkers, to augment this enigmatic realm of mental life. It is no less a topic than existence itself, an ontological exploration of a sense of being, or selfhood, or existence which is the requisite state of mind for contact with O.

Bion's theories

Bion crafted his theories in such a way that they might be used abstractly rather than merely to impart information or to assimilate already digested conclusions. These open or "empty" theories might then inspire the reader's awareness of his or her own questions, his own empty or open or "unsaturated" mind, to think his or her own thoughts. Bion's theories centre our attention on this experiential *process* of the mind, the mental space of a "container" *in relation to* its contents of sensations, feelings, dreams, and thoughts. This bi-modal relationship of container and contained (Bion, 1962a) is the foundation of the capacity to think. This theory might be considered to be his version of a libido theory, but with a basis in intrapsychic intercourse rather than physical intercourse. In the absence of this co-operative mental intercourse, a theory or idea is a sterile, concrete fact which can be stored in the mind as memory, but is no longer amenable to fluid use in creative thinking. Nietzsche (1886) described a similar idea, saying, "A thing explained is something we no longer have any concern with" (p. 92, Aphorism 80). (Bion talked about it as "dead but not yet buried imagination".)

What concerned Bion was not what was already known, but what remained unknown. He admitted that his theories did not always succeed in the ambitious task of facilitating new thoughts. Of course, the obstacles to communicating such ephemeral ideas militate against success, but we, as his audience, being human, naturally found it difficult to face the inherent limitations of our knowledge, and have, no doubt, often relied on the contents of his discoveries rather than braving that daunting and infinite new analytic space—O—to make discoveries on our own. Bion often remarked upon the pain of thinking and the widespread resistance to it, and so it is understandable that, as analysts, like all human beings, the primitive wish for an all-knowing expert or parent, a mentor, training analyst, or a God to give us answers, is easily activated. Bion was interested in thinking and so was constitutionally unsuited to the role of an all-knowing God. Rather, he provided an environment in which others might also be able to think. For Bion, thinking was a place of freedom and creative play which, like children's play, is serious, with an aim toward truth and mental development. It is the same space the artist inhabits in the creation of artistic truths.

Recollections of Bion

I set out to write a book from the heart as well as the mind. Psychoanalysis, after all, cannot be practised without access to both these aspects of human life, which together are the source of thinking. My intention, in part, was born of my personal impressions of Bion, for, although my experiences with him were limited in time spent, they have proved limitless in inspiration. This direct experience of Bion helped reveal to me something of how his theories were reflected in his personality, which provided me a different perspective on those theories. I thought, therefore, that it might be useful to present some recollections of my experience of Bion and the psychoanalytic milieu which existed during my brief studies with him in the 1970s. The title of this book, *Bion and Being: Passion and the Creative Mind*, refers, then, both to his theories and to the man himself, for even theoretical work is, in a sense, an autobiography of its creator. The change and foment in the psychoanalytic world during the 1970s often served as a dramatic enactment of Bion's theory of the catastrophic nature of change. This concurrence of theory and reality offered a view of Bion as an incarnation of that idea, for he was talking about the hatred of change, as he and his unfamiliar ideas were often becoming objects of hatred from his audiences. In my view, this sense of unity between him and his subject is one of the factors in the enduring influence of his ideas, for these ideas about the potential for mental integration were born of a mind capable of integration. I refrain from calling it "an integrated mind", for, as Bion makes clear, and as I try to describe in the book, the mind is engaged in a *process* of oscillation between integration and dis-integration throughout one's life (cf. Bion, 1970, Ps↔D). The very act of giving it a name—"mind"—erroneously suggests it is an entity, a thing, when in fact it is a process of mental energy with no fixed boundary.

Bion in Los Angeles

As most analysts know, Bion moved from England in 1967 and lived in Los Angeles for the last twelve years of his life, returning to England to retire in September of 1979. The shocking news that he had died less than two months later was devastating to all those throughout the world who appreciated his unusual mind and his role as a guide in the mysterious world of psychoanalytic thought. That world was changing significantly, in part due to his unique and revolutionary perspective. He had come to Los Angeles at the request of a group of Los Angeles analysts—Drs James Grotstein, John Linden, Bernard Bail, Arthur Malin, and Bernard Brandschaft—who had developed an interest in his work and the work of Melanie Klein. Bion and several Tavistock-trained British analysts, including Drs Albert Mason and Susanna Elmhirst Isaacs, infused the Los Angeles psychoanalytic community with new ideas. The reaction to this British invasion proved volatile and provoked a "war" within the local community, not unexpected given Bion's ideas about the behaviour of people in groups. Happily, however, the rancour and controversy did not silence the influx of new and interesting ideas which energised the analytic dialogue, inspiring invigorating discussion among analysts of all orientations, as well as candidates, students, and other mental health professionals.

I was a very young psychotherapist at the time, and while I was not directly involved in these wars, everyone knew of the ongoing controversy, foreshadowed in Britain's own earlier Freudian–Kleinian conflict. My primary direct contact with Bion centred around a private clinical seminar I arranged with him for myself and five other young therapists and analysts, and I attended all of his lectures at LAPSI, at UCLA's Neuropsychiatric Institute, and other places around Los Angeles.

In meeting Bion for our first interview in 1977, I commented how much his book, *Attention and Interpretation*, had meant to me. He seemed surprised, and said humbly, "I think I'm saying the same thing in every book." It reminded me of a statement by Ezra Pound in which he refers to the idea that each writer has in him only a "pint of truth" (Cookson, 1975, p. 34). This did not seem to me to be a devaluation of the limited message one conveyed in one's life, but a reflection of the idea that each person has his own idiosyncratic perspective on the world based on his own personality. Each person, that is, is a unique self. Of course, each thing one writes is not strictly a repetition, for as long that self continues to develop, so does one's capacity to deepen one's knowledge about that pint of truth, one's particular window on the world.

Hearing Bion lecture was always an eye-opening experience for me. However, what it actually opened my eyes to was how closed my mind was, how blind I really was to an area of experience, of the mind, of thinking, and of analysis, an area I could not then even fathom. I began to realise this from a combination of what Bion said and how he said it. His tone was simple, his ideas were complex, and his words had the ring of truth. Only upon hearing that sound did I become aware of how elusive it was, frequently missing from the words of many of my teachers and other respected analysts. However, I was also perplexed at what I heard from Bion as my mind opened up to a new depth, and to the depth of my ignorance. It was challenging, some found it frustrating and maddening, but many of us were exhilarated. Whatever he was saying, I sensed I wanted and needed to understand more about it and I was determined to find a way to do so. Although I did eventually find a way, the road was circuitous, painful, fascinating, and dangerous, as the quest for knowledge always is.

Clearly, Bion was a polarising figure. In part, paradoxically, I think it is because he represented wholeness. His theory of container and contained and his concept of "O—representing a transcendent numinous state of infinity, ultimate reality, absolute truth, the godhead—reflected the potential for a state of mental health and wholeness theretofore omitted from psychoanalytic discourse. Bion viewed the functions of feeling and thinking as dependent on, and necessary to, each other, but he did not only talk about it, he seemed to embody it. In his lectures he spoke slowly, gathering his thoughts in silence, often long silences, before he spoke. You could feel his presence and his courage as he took his time to think so that he might say something that had meaning in that moment, both to him and to the audience. One could almost "see" him thinking, consulting himself in the process, engaged in the reciprocal relationship between the mind as a container for the thoughts and feelings that might come to be contained there.

This was the work of thinking which, as Bion (1970) pointed out elsewhere, was a painful and usually hated enterprise, a point often proved by the audience reactions to him. In one of my seminars with him, our group seemed unable to think, without access to our own ideas or minds. As we all sat mute, I saw his anger flash, and after a long silence he declared, "Well, invention has failed us!"

In describing the difficulty of defining a psychoanalyst, Bion (1975) said, "You could say the mental experience and the sensuous experience have been making love to each other—hence the psychoanalyst" (p. 27). This probably describes as well as anything, the process of integration, or intercourse, of that relationship between container and contained. It is this that I sensed in him in these lectures, which resulted in the kind of striking presence described throughout the book as a sense of being.

Many in the audience became overtly hostile to Bion's slow, sometimes meandering responses to their questions, some spoke of him as "psychotic". They wanted answers, not a man pondering the question from different, often curious, perspectives, allowing his associations to lead him to a new thought. The rest of us were left to bear the frustration of trying to think for ourselves about issues for which there were no easy answers, or often no answers at all. His concept of O drew attention to the idea of an infinite unknown that is ultimately unknowable—feelings, thoughts, and mental states which, in analysis, as in life, cannot fully be grasped.

In lieu of experience, young therapists tend to rely on theories, and I was certainly no exception. No doubt this was part of the reason why Bion often advised those of us who attended the clinical seminar at his home to, "Keep your questions in good repair" (Bion, 1977d). One was better off being armed with questions and a way to ponder them rather than an arsenal of answers to clutter one's mind and prevent authentic dynamic thought. To make his point, he often repeated Maurice Blanchot's statement, *"La réponse est le malheur de la question"* ("The answer is the misfortune [or illness] of the question"). Many of Bion's words in his lectures and in our seminar have stuck with me all these years, as has the memory of Mrs Bion's delicious cakes, which were graciously laid out for us with coffee each week.

Dr Bion's consulting room was in a brick medical building at 435 N. Bedford Drive in Beverly Hills, the same building in which I was then sub-renting the office of Dr Marcia da Silva, a Brazilian analyst who, along with her analyst husband, had temporarily relocated to Los Angeles to study with, and be analysed by, Bion. I have long since moved to my own office one block west, but the Bedford building remains heavily populated by psychoanalysts and psychotherapists. The city has changed since then, however. The now famously posh Rodeo Drive, two blocks east of Bion's old building, at that time had a hardware store, a bookstore, and other homely businesses on a street now graced only by the likes of Prada and Tiffany's. There were also at least three bookstores within the small radius that is Beverly Hills, which now has a shocking and shameful *none*. One of these was a psychoanalytic bookshop, a small dusty store at the front of which an equally dusty looking old man sat reading at an old wooden desk. He rarely spoke, and when he did his voice, coloured by a Hungarian accent, was quiet and weak, as if emanating from a distant place. He was dour and downright creepy at times, and I am sure I failed to appreciate the fact of having a psychoanalytic bookstore in our midst when, to my knowledge, such stores are now rare anywhere at all. It was from this man that I bought, among other things, Bion's books, including the slender hard-bound copies of *Learning From Experience* and *Elements of Psychoanalysis*, published by Basic Books in 1962 and 1963, respectively. In the upper right corners of each of the title pages I can still see the old man's faint pencil marks, which read, "1st edition".

As I wrote a cheque for my purchases, this usually curmudgeonly man commented on my interest in Bion's work. Obviously impressed by Bion, he added, "He comes in here all the time, mostly to buy poetry." After a few more words on the subject, I left. That was it, a conversation that could not have been more mundane, but which I have remembered for thirty-five years, for in that moment I sensed our common recognition of what a rare thing it was to have a genius in our midst.

Hinshelwood (2010) makes the point that Bion's concept of O necessitated a complete revision of what analysis is and how people learn; it represented an awareness of the limits of scientific knowledge and the analyst's reliance on intuition as its primary technique. Understanding this aspect of the mind requires the analyst to reach beyond knowledge gained through awareness of the senses to the numinous realm of O, which Bion likens to Kant's thing-in-itself and Plato's pure Forms. It is a mystical state (Grotstein (2007, p. 24) calls Bion "the first to establish the new 'mystical science of psychoanalysis'"), the functions of which will be discussed at length in Chapters Five and Eight. Bion saw this state as essential to the practical work of psychoanalysis, but it also has much in common with the states of mind which fuel the creation of art, poetry, literature, music, dance, etc. The artist uses paint, canvas, marble, etc., musicians use sound and silence, the dancer uses his own body and the space through which he moves, and writers use the words and music of speech, but through these various physical modes, each artist must find a way to express these otherwise intangible metaphysical realities. Since psychoanalysts rely primarily on words (but also, as Bion pointed out, on silence), in Chapters Three, Four, and Six I will explore the potential as well as the limits of language to fulfil this task. Our theoretical language often distances us from an experience of the mysteries we are called upon to feel and express to our patients, and so I will enlist the aid of creative artists whose works offer more experiential expressions of these theories in the languages of the arts. The aim is to help reactivate the feelings of mystery and passion that underlie our theories, to connect us to their emotional roots, and to our own.

My own life as a poet has helped me to understand my clinical work from that experiential perspective, and so I will use excerpts from my own poems, as well as those of Rilke, Shakespeare, Dickinson, Cummings, and others, to examine Bion's theories from these different vertices. The works of philosophers and literary artists like Plato, Beckett, and Nietzsche, and visual artists such as Matisse, Picasso, de Kooning and others, will also add other perspectives on these experiences.

After Bion's death Meltzer (1981) wrote,

> . . . the quality that distinguished Wilfred Bion, and which marks his passing from us with such serious consequences for psychoanalysts . . . was his capacity to tolerate caesura after caesura, to weather what he called 'Catastrophic Change'. (Meltzer, 1981, p. 13)

This capacity seemed a function of Bion's fervid and enduring curiosity and the fact that he was possessed of the mental strength to continue being curious and to continue observing "until a pattern emerged". He often referred to this advice from Charcot (quoted admiringly by Freud), ". . . to look at the same things again and again until they themselves begin to speak" (Freud, 1914d, p. 22). In this need to keep the mind open to new answers, Bion would no doubt agree with Nietzsche's (1878) maxim, "Convictions are more dangerous enemies of truth than lies" (p. 179).

For Bion, analytic work was more about the questions one asked than the answers one found. An endeavour like analysis, whose focus is the non-sensual life of the mind, cannot offer the same kind of phenomenological proof as sciences based on the senses, but, despite the limitations, the openness of the curious mind provides another kind of truth. Bion served as a fitting model for the idea that one can do no better than to keep on looking with curiosity, intuition, discipline, and patience, in the hope of finding as many new questions as he did throughout his life and, with any luck, maybe a few partial, fleeting answers as well.

If we are right in thinking we have minds we shall have to do some-thing about them.

Wilfred Bion (1975, p. 50)

CHAPTER ONE

"O": Bion's "truth instinct"*

> "Out beyond ideas of wrongdoing and rightdoing
> there is a field. I'll meet you there"
>
> (Rumi, 2003, p. 123)

In Bion's lexicon, the "field" in this excerpt from Rumi's poem is "O". It provides an apt description of Bion's most mysterious idea, representing absolute truth and the state of mind necessary to apprehend it. It is a place of experiential awareness rather than judgement. In a way, Rumi's words might be an appropriate invitation to our analytic patients, except for the fact that at the beginning of treatment patients are usually unable to meet us in that "field" beyond wrongdoing and rightdoing, for they are often caught up in primitive judgements and confusions which make such a meeting impossible. As analysts, however, we have to be able to join the patient without judgement in whatever field he or she currently resides—in their central essential experience—O.

---

*A term coined by Grotstein (2007, p. 139).

O is the lynchpin of Bion's ideas around which all of his theories cohere: reverie, alpha function, thoughts without a thinker, container–contained, the suspension of memory and desire, Ps↔D etc., and so an emotional understanding of this idea becomes essential in understanding his work. One might view the metaphysical experience of O as the "selected fact" (Bion, 1962a) that organises and helps make sense of Bion's theories. It corresponds to the inherent human attribute of a fundamental need for truth, which Grotstein (2007, p. 139) referred to as the idea of a "truth instinct" present throughout Bion's work. In terms of clinical work, Bion ascribed central importance to O as the foundation of psychoanalytic practice, the necessary psychoanalytic perspective upon which the success of analytic work depends.

This chapter offers an overview of ideas about O that will be more fully explored throughout the book. One writes about O, however, knowing the futility of trying to describe something that is ultimately indescribable. "[O] stands for the absolute truth in and of any object; it is assumed that this cannot be known by any human being" (Bion, 1970, p. 30). Bion also speaks of it as a ". . . central and basic point . . . [which] I have tried to signify by a letter O—to signify it, merely to indicate that this is 'some thing'; but what it is I do not know" (Bion, 1975, p. 30).

Like the metaphorical "field" in Rumi's poem, there is no such place; it is a state of mind, a state of flux. In psychological terms, it relates to selfhood or being, also in a constant state of flux or becoming. In theological terms, it is the spirit or soul or God. Of course, this state of "being", a quality used to describe both material and immaterial existence, is no less difficult to describe. The word "being" itself is a gerund, an "action noun", which has properties of both noun and verb, so we might say that one can be engaged in an *act* of being while in a mental *process* of being. In terms of its relationship to O, it can simultaneously reflect both active and passive states of mind, integrating those aspects of one's material (outer, physical) and immaterial (inner or metaphysical) existence. Bion's ideas about a Language of Achievement (below, Chapter Six) demonstrate this, language that is potent enough to represent a prelude to action, which I would say is a function of that integrated state of being.

Elusive O

There is a river in Arizona called the Hassayampa, whose name derives from a Native American word denoting disappearance and reappearance. The river goes underground in places, then resurfaces in others. It is analogous to the oscillations in the mind when one relinquishes conscious awareness as one's ego "disappears" into the dreams of an unconscious realm. One enters that dream-like, semi-conscious reverie as if swept along in the currents of a suddenly appearing river, then resurfaces into consciousness armed with emotional "information" from that realm to which one otherwise lacks access. Access to O depends upon this dream-like state of mind, which presents one's raw primitive experiences to be transformed into thought (cf. Bion, 1963, reverie, alpha function).

The story told by the Yavapai tribe regarding this sometimes "invisible" river is that once one has stepped into it, he can never again tell the truth (James, 1917, p. 363). It is an interesting myth in view of the fear of the unconscious as a menacing place of obscurity and confusion, and it raises the question as to whether one can never tell the truth again, or, on the contrary, that *only* in contact with that obscure realm is one capable of telling the deeper truth. Psycho-analytically, this reflects the two views of dreams, either as a distortion of reality as Freud's theory of dreams suggests, or a means to more essential truth, as Bion's idea of dreaming upholds.

Bion clearly expressed the ongoing nature of dreaming in waking life as central to processing truth and raw emotional experience. He described a non-pathological state of hallucinosis that is "always present but overlaid by other phenomena which screen it" (1970, p. 36). Dreams are obscured from our awareness by the myriad distractions of external reality, all the perceptions of a sensuous world that are suspended as we sleep. We continue dreaming throughout the day, we just do not see our dreams, like the stars which are invisible to us during the day in the sun's blinding light. For the analyst, opening the mind's "eye" to this invisible reality *while awake* depends upon temporarily closing the mind to the distractions of the senses. One facilitates this by suspending memory, desire, and understanding (Bion, 1970). This temporary suspension of the senses as one connects with a dream-like metaphysical state in waking life can give rise to terrifying feelings of loss of control, since our senses help ground us in the familiar identities of our physical lives.

There is evidence of the revolutionary aspect of Bion's work in his description of the dangers of this discipline, and the resulting experience of contact with O as "an attack on the ego" (1970, p. 48). Suspending memory, desire, and understanding, he says, gives rise to a state of mind similar to that which occurs in severely regressed patients, and he, therefore, advocates this procedure "only for the analyst whose own analysis has been carried at least far enough for the recognition of paranoid schizoid and depressive positions" (p. 47 fn).

Metaphysical and religious aspects of O

Symington and Symington (1996) describe the metaphysical or religious meaning in Bion's idea of O as providing a fundamentally different foundation to psychoanalytic thought, which is foreign to the works of Klein or Freud. The concept of O first appeared in Bion's work in *Transformations* (1965) and in *Attention and Interpretation* (1970), causing some of his colleagues to believe he had gone mad (Symington & Symington, 1996). Introducing a metaphysical sense of an infinite unknowable reality to the scientific world of psychoanalysis dealt yet another disturbing blow to man's egocentric view. It indicated, as had Freud's idea of an unconscious, that man was not the master of his own mind. Bion's idea went further, however, as the concept of O introduced questions about the possibility of knowledge itself. He likened it to Heisenberg's "uncertainty principle" (Bion, 1992, p. 263), which suggested that quantum physicists were not dealing merely with obstacles to their existing methods or current knowledge, but with the limits of knowledge itself. In the world of physics, it was learnt that one could not simultaneously chart the location and momentum of a particle, not because the proper equipment had not been invented to measure it, but because the act of measuring itself interfered with the other measurement. The observer, in other words, presented a disturbance to the field being observed. Similarly, in the mind, the concept of O suggested that it was not the absence of analytic knowledge, but the fact that we are dealing with an ultimately unknowable internal universe. In addition, the observer—the analyst—changes the field of observation in the complex relationship to the patient.

Scientist–inventor, Barry Lebost, describes how scientific truth has suffered from human beings putting themselves at a central position in relation to the observable universe. Even the greatest scientists, he says, have viewed the world as invariant, based on an assumption that the visible world accurately depicts the world that is. He upholds that this kind of "centre stage observance" blinds people to the more complex and dynamic variant world beyond our awareness, and that scientific conclusions have been drawn based on these erroneous assumptions. Lebost (2008) writes, "Physical truth will never be understood until the phenomenon of observer invariance is fully accounted for" (p. xii). Einstein, for instance, saw the speed of light as invariant. However, with the invention of the Chandra X-ray telescope in 1999, new information about the expansion and acceleration of the universe became available, information to which Einstein could not have had access. Based on these findings, conclusions drawn from the erroneous assumption of an invariant speed of light proved untrue. Lebost makes the following observation regarding the expanding, accelerating universe, a phenomenon we cannot see, but which we now know exists.

> A new paradigm is emerging that proves that humankind and all living things exist in two realities. The first is the invariant world that we are familiar with, the one in which we think we live. It is what we see . . . The second is the true universe that is in a relentless pursuit to become larger, a place where all yardsticks continuously become longer at a faster and faster rate. This dynamic and variant world is invisible to all observers because all living observers are integral members of the universal accelerating frame and have been granted no outside references for comparison. When we finally accept the new world we will have taken a giant step into reality. We will have learned that much goes on around us without human awareness. (Lebost, 2011)

This idea of an outside frame of reference is inherently mysterious. How can one observe from outside one's own frame of reference? How can we see what we cannot see? And yet, this is the implicit proposal in Bion's concept of O. The analyst is called upon to use a different level of his or her perceptual apparatus, without which assumptions continue to be made based on erroneous beliefs in an invariant world. One is asked to enter a realm of mystical knowledge beyond memory, desire, and the understanding gained from physical perceptions experienced through the senses. In this mental state of at-one-ment, one's perceptions extend past one's known self and personal experience. Bion makes it clear, however, that this is not incompatible with scientific knowledge, and he includes scientists in his description of the mystic. "Newton is the outstanding example of such a man; his mystical and religious preoccupations have been dismissed as an aberration when they should be considered as the matrix from which his mathematical formulations evolved" (Bion, 1970, p. 64).

Bion's idea of O, though derived from Freud's theory of the unconscious, goes further by including the idea of a transcendent unknowable realm of primal proto-mental knowledge, vestiges, perhaps, of pre-natal experience. It is akin to the realm depicted in Jung's archetypes, which are seen to "exist in the unconscious as undifferentiated symbols" (McGuire & Hull, 1977, p. 216), and the idea of the collective unconscious, described by Jung as "everything that precedes the personal history of the human being" (ibid., p. 231). The Oedipal myth, Jung explained, was one example of such an archetype, stored in the collective unconscious of the race. Bion (1978) viewed Jung's ideas of archetypes and the collective unconscious as expressions of the same unaltered fundamental mind he described as proto-mental memories (p. 4). O describes both that unnameable unrepresentable external reality Grotstein describes as "the world as it is, the universe without representations" (2011, private conversation) and the individual's primal internal preconception of that natural world. The attempt to experience the relationship between these two aspects of O is the essential work of analysis. It is based on an experience of separateness that, paradoxically, is the foundation of union and passion.

Philosophy, art, religion

Although Bion introduced the metaphysical or mystical idea of O to psychoanalysis, the experience it represents is certainly nothing new. Philosophers, poets, theologians, and artists have examined this state of mind since the beginning of history. It is also the essential basis of creative work of all kinds, and Bion recognised the common task of analysts and artists in expressing the elusive metaphysical truths beyond the senses. "It would be useful if we could recognize that all these various disciplines—music, painting, psycho-analysis and so on ad infinitum—are engaged on the same search for truth" (Bion, 1978, p. 43).

At moments of inspiration, the individual inhabits a state of being, although it is more accurate to say that he is inhabited *by* that state of being to which he succumbs, a feeling of being taken over by a force beyond his control. As if swept up and carried along by that suddenly emerging Hassayampa River, this process of being connects one to an instinctual level of truth and life; exhilarating in its potential for knowledge and creative inspiration, it also inspires fear and resistance at the lack of control over one's own emotional experience. Alluding to this fear, Bion wrote, "Resistance is resistance to O. Resistance operates because it is feared that reality is imminent" (1965, p. 127). The nature of this reality beyond common everyday reality will be more fully investigated in Chapters Three and Four.

O and morality

In concordance with the notion of Rumi's field "beyond wrongdoing and rightdoing", Bion (1965) writes, "[O] is not good or evil; it cannot be known, loved, or hated" (p. 139). His definitions of O as ultimate reality, absolute truth, the godhead, portray a level of reality requiring a more evolved mental state to make contact with it. It corresponds to Nietzsche's (1886) idea of a new system of values "beyond good and evil", which would require an *Übermensch* or superman, a "new philosopher" or "new psychologist" to think it. The task of these "genuine philosophers" (p. 136, sec. 211) was to "overcome the entire past" (ibid.) in order to create a new future. Philosophers, and society in general, were seen by Nietzsche as having lacked an essential awareness, and he lamented those past and current "philosophical laborers" whose job had been to force the existing stores of knowledge and long dominant values into comprehensible formulae. These ideas of Nietzsche, Rumi, and Bion in the varied disciplines of philosophy, poetry, and psychoanalysis, all denote a level of knowledge beyond societal judgement. This "new philosopher", whose attributes are more fully examined in Chapter Eight, needed to think for himself beyond the beliefs of the prevailing customs, according to his individual mind. This included the capacity for knowledge of one's inner intentions, an idea of Nietzsche's that presaged Freud's theory of the unconscious, the hidden thoughts and intentions which determined behaviour.

O and the Übermensch

Nietzsche's *Übermensch* represents an ideal, a human potential for mental capacities still in the process of developing. First mentioned in *Thus Spoke Zarathustra* (Nietzsche, 1885a), the *Übermensch* was a Superman of noble tastes, the aim of human development, while man in his current state was something in need of being surmounted. The need for awareness of primitive emotional life contained in psycho-analytic thought is reflected in Nietzsche's idea that man's mental evolution would be dependent on a vision able to span the heights and depths of human experience, a marriage of the human and the divine, of primal and higher states of mind. "Man is a rope", he wrote, "fastened between animal and Superman—a rope over an abyss" (sec. 4, p. 43).

Bion also spoke about the need for further mental development in order to be able to experience and communicate metaphysical states of mind. While thinking might appear to be something everyone can do, both Bion and Nietzsche are describing a kind of thinking dependent upon the fulfilment of a higher mental potential. Thinking, Bion (1962b) writes, ". . . is embryonic even in the adult and has yet to be developed fully by the race" (p. 85). For Nietzsche, this new thinker is described as the future of man, "a man of tomorrow and the day after tomorrow . . . His enemy was ever the ideal of today" (sec. 212, p. 137).

Nietzsche's statement can also be understood with reference to Gertrude Stein's notion that the genius is someone who lives in a future which already exists in the present, and which he or she is able to put forth in a new vision. Those who cannot see it are still living in the past, their knowledge based on assumptions that they force to fit into old preconceived notions of reality. This idea resonates with Bion's (1970) description of the role of the mystic or genius, whose new ideas are at odds with the values of the society or group and so pose a threat to its homogeneity and its survival. By all these defini-tions, the *Übermensch*, the mystic, and the genius are characterised by the capacity for contact with the mystical state of "at-one-ment"—O—developed through the integration of reason and primitive emotion.

The genius is able to intuit and create an image for an impending future that for him already exists. He or she already lives in a reality informed by a new vision, an as yet unknown and uncontained cultural reality which the artist or genius finds a way to represent. Bion acknowledged the importance of this when he cited Nietzsche's idea that "the function of a nation is to produce one genius" (Bion, 1975, p. 58).

Nietzsche describes the frustrations of trying to make contact with this evolved state.

> Who is this then, this Wisdom? . . . One thirsts for her and is not satisfied, one looks at her through veils . . . Is she fair? I know not! . . . She is changeable and defiant. . . . Perhaps she is wicked and false, and in everything a wench . . . And again [contemplating this] I seemed to sink into the unfathomable. (Nietzsche, 1885a, p. 132)

The genius, or *Übermensch*, capable even of intermittent balance on that bridge between man and "God" is possessed of a mind able to experience creative passion, with its "progeny" of new thoughts and ideas. That union is a celebration of passion, a quality present throughout Nietzsche's work and typified by the expressiveness of his poetic style. This mental balance is described in Bion's important statement about genius, not as a fixed state, but as a *process* of thinking, a process so challenging that it is sometimes enough to drive one mad.

> Genius has been said to be akin to madness. It would be more true to say that psychotic mechanisms require a genius to manipulate them in a manner adequate to promote growth or life (which is synonymous with growth). (1970, p. 63, original parentheses).

The artist's O

In *Memoir of the Future* (1991), Bion wrote, "Disguised as fiction the truth occasionally slipped through" (p. 302). Freud pointed out the familiarity that artists have with this realm of the unconscious, even admitting in a letter to Roman Rolland, "It is easier for you [writers] than for us [psychoanalysts] to read the human soul" (E. Freud, 1960, p. 389). Freud's statement helps us to see the difference between his perspective and Bion's with his focus on the unknowable O, where the analyst, like the artist, requires a relationship to more essential and primitive modes of experience.

The new truths derived from contact with that numinous realm encounter harsh resistance both inside and outside the analyst's consulting room. The history of art is filled with examples of negative reactions to the new and unknown. In 1907, for instance, "Les Demoiselles d'Avignon" was met with scorn and horror as Picasso shifted from a classical realistic view of the figure to an emotionally driven, idiosyncratic vision. The angular, somewhat menacing shapes of these women departed drastically from traditional standards of aesthetic beauty. With faces like African masks depicting prostitutes in a bordello, its primitive nature appalled many art lovers, critics, and even Picasso's close associates. His vision, expressing something beyond physical reality, brought them face to face with an unknown metaphysical realm (Rubin, 1980).

About the artistic expression of metaphysical states, Matisse wrote, "There is an inherent truth which must be disengaged from the outward appearance of the object to be represented. This is the only truth that matters" (Read, 1974, p. 44). The appearance of a painting perceived through the senses—shapes, colours, composition, etc.—differs from the artist's essential inner experience, which enters and suffuses the work through more mysterious means. Matisse is a particularly "truthful" artist when it comes to creating emotionally authentic works that imbue a feeling of immediacy and inevitability, of something which had to emerge from that artist at that moment. They are created in a moment of *being*, and if we, as viewers, are open to it, that feeling of authenticity is recreated in us so that we, too, experience a moment of being, a moment of our deeper selves. While such works might not seem familiar or traditionally beautiful, they have an aura of beauty nonetheless, in the sense of Keats' (1820) equation, "Truth is Beauty, Beauty, Truth . . ." (p. 253).

While art, philosophy, religion, and analysis provide different perspectives on the same truth, there is a blurring of the boundaries between them. Matisse said, "My approach is not aesthetic. I want to eliminate what is not essential and what is therefore detrimental to the hypnotic power of the image" (Gilot, 1990, p. 77). That hypnotic power is an expression of the artist's contact with, in Bion's terms, O, that higher, more essential truth synonymous with beauty. In the extract below, Matisse tells something of this experience, which is also a good description of O.

> In art, the truth, the real, begins when one no longer understands anything, and an energy remains in you sufficiently strong, compressed, charged . . . One must offer it with the greatest humility, totally pure, candid, with a seemingly empty brain, in a state analogous to that with which someone approaches [a] Saint for communion. You must put everything you know behind you to protect the freshness of Instinct. (Matisse, 1947, pp. 16–18)

O as being and non-being

Matisse's description, like an experience of O, is a capacity to embrace a feeling of nothingness or non-being, but this "empty brain" differs from a nihilistic state which is antithetical to the existence of the mind. Rather, it denotes the existence of a mind with sufficient space in which something new might come into existence. Nietzsche (1878) suggests this idea in his description of the writer's state of mind in relation to the compelling force of the new idea. "When his work opens its mouth, the author has to shut his" (p. 245, Aphorism 140). When inspiration comes, one must be willing to relinquish one's known self as one enters that empty space. Paradoxically, this essential emptiness, with its sense of non-being, provides the space in which is contained one's sense of being.

Bion states, "The rule that a thing cannot both be and not be is inadequate" (1965, p. 102). This intercourse between being and non-being is expressed in Bion's discussion of the "no-thing", which, in fact, represents a thing, or, rather, the space for an absent thing. It is an *idea* or *thought* of a thing, originally the thought of an absent mother, which, according to Bion, is the origin of thought itself. It is a mind that can act as a container for the thought which has suddenly come into existence to be thought.

These ideas resonate with the first of Rilke's (1912b) *Duino Elegies*. In the extract below, Rilke describes the kind of listening one needs if one is going to hear "God's" voice.

> Not that you could bear hearing God's voice—oh no.
> But listen to that soft blowing . . .
> that endless report that grows out of silence.
>
> (Rilke, 1912b, p. 23)

O, too, grows out of silence, as the analyst listens to the patient to hear that which is *not* said, that which presents itself so softly it can barely be made out. Like poetry, it is written between the lines. One listens in that space between being and non-being, and as Rilke's poem continues, he reflects, not only on death, but on these mental states of being and non-being.

> Of course it is odd to live no more on the earth . . .
> to be held no more by hands that can never relax
> for fear they will drop you,
> and even to put your name to one side like a broken toy.
> Strange to wish wishes no longer.
> Strange to see things that seemed to belong together
> floating in every direction.
> It's very hard to be dead
> and you try to make up for lost time
> till slowly you start to get whiffs of eternity.
> But the living are wrong in the sharp distinctions they make.
> Angels, it seems, don't always know if they're moving
> among the living or the dead.
> The drift of eternity drags all the ages of man
> through both of those spheres
> and its sound rises over them both.
>
> (ibid., pp. 24–25)

Death is rendered here as an experience that is part of life, that is, mental life, and how wrong the living are to make such sharp distinctions between life and death. The mind in contact with O, beyond sensual reality, is essentially that experience of "no longer living on the earth", having suspended its physical earthly awareness. If one dares to let oneself drop into that uncontrolled dream-like state, one might then have contact with the life of the spirit where one may hear that divine and quiet voice. One allows oneself, as he later writes, to be "weaned from the things of this world" (p. 26). This temporary "death" of the self is in the service of a far more vast and expansive self. Rilke even describes the fragmentation that comes of contact with this level of primitive mental functioning—"things that seemed to belong together [are] floating in every direction"—an experience very familiar to the analyst in contact with O.

In psychoanalytic terms, this is a descent into the paranoid–schizoid position (Klein, 1946). It differs, however, from the infant's lack of integration, for it now has a background of mental development that significantly changes the experience. Still, the difficult discipline of suspending ego functions of memory, desire, and understanding allows access to that challenging state of dis-integration which is one aspect of contact with O. Again, in Bion's (1975) view, it is central to analytic work, as he saw memory and desire as "breaches in the analytic frame of mind" (p. 38). Experiences of mental death and life are continuous throughout life. As Rilke wrote, ". . . all the ages of man . . . [are dragged] / through both of those spheres", an idea echoed in Bion's (1970) idea of the ongoing fluctuations between primitive experience and the more organised state of the depressive position (cf. Bion, 1970, Ps↔D).

Like the analysand's, and the analyst's, fear of being lowered into this mysterious unknown, Rilke's line (above, p. 11), "Not that you could bear hearing God's voice—oh no . . .", describes the fear of suspending contact with the sensual world in favour of this numinous realm. One braves these dangers, however, because of a need for truth, which is felt to be essential to one's existence.

> But we who have need of those huge mysteries,
> we who can sometimes draw up from wellsprings of sadness
> rejoicing and progress, how could we exist without them?
> Is the old tale pointless that tells how music began
> in the midst of the mourning for Linos,
> piercing the arid numbness and,
> in that stunned space where an almost godlike youth
> had suddenly stopped existing,
> made emptiness vibrate in ways that thrill us,
> comfort us, help us now?
>
> (Rilke, 1912b, p. 26)

This is the emptiness of O as well, which is not, in fact, empty, but is filled with the un-sensible—the invisible, formless, inaudible, odourless, tasteless energy of being—which the poet can potentiate in the form of a poem, or the analyst in the form of an interpretation. One braves the "emptiness" because of the feeling of wholeness and authenticity that can develop out of it.

The wish for non-being: clinical considerations

The patient's desire for a state of non-being is usually very different from the emptiness Matisse described as the origin of authentic creative work, or the analyst's capacity for O. There is an old joke written by comedy writer Harry Crane, who said, "My wife left me after thirty years . . . she said she wanted to go 'find' herself. Such a great discovery it ain't gonna be!" While more amusing, this is not unlike the problem we face with our patients. If they have the courage to stick with the difficult journey of analysis, they may actually find access to their authentic emotional selves. In my experience, it is never what they expected, and they are rarely happy to face what they have to face on this journey. Beginning to experience authentic feelings, they become angry and suspicious of the analyst, sometimes for months, even years, for destroying their illusions of control over their internal and external worlds.

The analyst might assume he or she is working to help the patient experience his feelings, but the patient's unconscious assumption is often that the analyst will excise the painful feelings like a surgeon. Having hoped to be "cured" of feelings, the patient is frightened and angry to find that there is no cure for being human, and that their feelings are, in fact, more intense.

Clinical example: "Mark"

"Mark", a man in his forties, is in the process of an emotional awakening. He is terrified to discover in himself the feelings of an exquisitely sensitive baby, a breakthrough he does not appreciate, as it feels to him like a breakdown of the personality previously thought to be his real self. His mother left him with care-takers at birth, returning after a month. In addition, he was sexually abused, and later tortured, by a cruelly jealous older sister. His father was absent and his mother was unable to cope with her own or her children's emotional needs. Mark's belief that he could be cured of feelings was a "lie" he told himself in an attempt to endure these traumas of his early life. He has lived in the phantasy of a sort of foetal oneness meant to protect him from the pain of his enormous needs in an environment that could not meet them. These unconscious lies can prove erosive to the treatment, but, after years of deadness followed by years of anger at me for the pain he started to feel, he has now begun to tolerate very painful feel-ings of need. He has even begun to see some value in having "real emotions," so that, like Pinocchio, he might become "a real live boy".

> Mark dreamt of being in a parking garage. He had to take a number as one might in a store, but when he did a structure collapsed on a station wagon and sliced off a baby's head inside. Horrified, Mark screamed to a doctor, "Save the baby! Save the baby!" The doctor sewed the head back on and Mark said, "Thank God for modern medicine!" He knew, how-ever, that all the baby could do was run around. The head was essentially dead.

The patient remarked that his mother had a station wagon when he was a boy. Having long ago anaesthetised his feelings as protection from the unbearable realities he had endured early on, Mark had essentially lost his "head", his capacities to feel and to develop his mind. Like the baby with the severed head, he had created his own modern medicine, which made him appear to be a real live boy, able to "run around", but emotionally dead. In his mind, I am a confusing mixture of a helpful but ineffective doctor, for he has been under the impression that I would be that amazing modern doctor who would sew him together so he would not have to feel those terrible feelings. As his current breakdown/breakthrough of feelings disabuses him of this illusion, he often feels out of control, terrified, and desperate for my help. In the middle of this mental rebirth of these painful emotional states he believed he had severed, he cannot tell if he is dying or coming to life, or just what kind of a doctor I am. If I am not saving his false self from pain, am I, in fact, "killing" that already dead self by causing him pain? I appear to be doing a very bad job, for, in this confusing clash of states of non-being and incipient being, he cannot distinguish that it is the "dead" self that is coming to life as his authentic feeling self is born.

After I relayed this basic confusion to Mark, he recalled his older sister having once severed the head of his favourite teddy bear, then tearing it into tiny pieces. It was a fitting description of the fragmen-tation Mark experienced as his authentic self was splintered and lost to him, with no one to hear him or gather together the bits of terror, confusion, and rage he could not feel in his severed head. Under-standably, his rage at me was fierce, lasting almost two years, as his emotional self was coming to life. At the point of this dream, however, his despair and desperation were inescapable, for he had realised that he had run around mindless his whole life, while emotionally encrypted behind an impenetrable wall.

Mark's courage and determination in the face of genuine terror were evidence to me of his constitutional need for truth, what Bion (1992) described as "a disposition for truth" (p. 262). In my experience, this is more rare than we, as analysts, would like to think, for, while everyone theoretically wants truth and enlightenment, few seem to want it in reality when it reaches this point of unrelenting confusion about who or what or where one is. In this context, we might under-stand Mark's taking a number in the dream as getting his turn at a life that never came, at which he now has another chance.

These states of non-being are common. We can see in our patients, and in ourselves, the resistances to life, to knowledge, to feeling, to experience, to O. The desire for the death of the self is reflected in an unconscious preference for lies over truth, and the "decision", often made in the earliest days of life, to live a lie which denies the mind and the existence of inner life.

Neruda laments that which is lost in this process.

> Why was I not born mysterious?
> Why did I grow up without companions?
> Who ordered me to tear down
> the doors of my own pride?
> And who went out to live for me
> when I was sleeping or sick? . . .
> (Neruda, 1974 , p. 59)

It is a telling description of the development of a false self, which ensues in the wake of early emotional trauma. It gives rise to the enduring confusion between love and hate described by Rosenfeld (1978), and the confusion between mental life and death by which Mark and so many others are plagued. The battle between truth and lies is a battle royale between the death of the self and the possibility of being.

CHAPTER TWO

Self and other: passion and play in analysis and art

"A person with talent hits the target no one else can hit. A genius hits the target no one else can see"

(Young, 2005, p. 126)

The earliest meaning of the word "passion" (from Old French "pati") was to suffer or endure. The meaning of strong emotion or desire was not included until 1250, and by the 1500s it also carried the meaning of sexual love (Barnhart, 1988). In the context of analytic work, however, Bion defines passion in a particular way.

I mean the term [passion] to represent an emotion experienced with intensity and warmth though without any suggestion of violence. . . . Awareness of passion is not dependent on sense. For senses to be active, only one mind is necessary: passion is evidence that two minds are linked and that there cannot possibly be fewer than two minds if passion is present. (Bion, 1963, p. 13)

By this definition, passion requires an awareness of and capacity for separateness, the awareness of an other as well as a sense of one's own existence. Passion is, therefore, a function of being. It is a capacity for separate existence, however, which includes the capacity to lose one's self in the other, that temporary "death" of the self beyond the limitations of a split or splintered ego. In Bion's view, passion is a basic analytic element, and the experience of the presence or absence of this sense of passion in the patient provides the analyst with a sense of the patient's emotional existence or non-existence.

Implicit in Christ's Passion—his destiny to suffer the sins of mankind—is the need of a saviour to suffer man's sins *for* him. This gives us a good indication of the difficulties people have in experiencing their guilt and, more generally, feelings of any kind. Since it is feelings that give one a sense of being alive, the inability to feel them points to the lack of mental integration which obstructs one's sense of authentic existence. The resulting sense of emotional non-existence reflects the mental state Bion (1970) described in some patients who can "experience pain but not suffering" (p. 19). Emotional pain that is not suffered has been projected, split off, anaesthetised, etc., and cannot then be experienced by the individual as a mental state. Rather, it is felt as something external to the self, a pain imposed from without by a hostile someone or something else, and that precludes the experiences of passion and being.

Bion's ideas of passion and the analytic couple have similarities to ideas about intersubjectivity and the "analytic third" (Ogden, 1996). Grotstein credits Bion with having established these ideas about the analytic couple, in which intersecting subjective experiences are created in the relationship between both members of the couple, and create something new between them. Grotstein (2007) writes, "Bion has been accorded the role of the one who introduced intersubjectivity (the indivisibility of the two-person relationship) into Kleinian, as well as general, analytic thinking" (pp. 37–38). Bion often clearly expressed this idea in his statement, "The patient is not really interested in himself, nor is he interested in the analyst, but in the bit in between" (1977b). The analyst, too, is interested in this "bit in between", the co-mingling of mental energies in which a transformation can occur in each of the people willing to bear the truth of their shared existence, to the mutual benefit of both. Bion's idea of a "transformation in O" refers to the ability to meet in this metaphysical realm beyond the senses and the effects of so doing, which facilitate a sense of oneness beyond the boundaries of each individual self. It is the complex, ineffable state of separateness and the capacity for an experience of oneness with the other.

The ineffability of this kind of relationship raises the question about who or what is actually meeting in any psychoanalytic session (or anywhere else) at any given time. The capacity to entertain this question about the meaning of the self and of separateness, of passion and meaning and a sense of being, is of central importance in the analyst's practical clinical work. As we will see here, it is also a question of the presence or absence of a capacity to play.

Child's play: the creation of the self

Winnicott's (1971) idea of a combined infant–mother which cannot be distinguished in the infant's mind is described in adult relationships in Buber's idea of "I–Thou". Buber (1970) writes, "there is no I as such, but only the I of the basic word I–You . . . [This] basic word can only be spoken with one's whole being" (p. 54). This, too, reflects the sense of passion in the simultaneous awareness of separateness and at-one-ment with the other. Bion (1975) described it in mathematical terms with reference to set theory, where two intersecting sets create a "set which one could say is 'you and me'" (p. 43). Only in the achievement of a capacity for separateness can one transcend one's separateness in order to bond in this way. The alternative is an undifferentiated state of primitive fusion, either of the healthy infant as yet developmentally incapable of separateness, or the pathological fusion driven by a retreat from emotional life and attachment.

Like dreams, the child's play creates the inner world of images borrowed from external experience. This symbolic and imagistic language of the inner world is also the basis of language we use to communicate inner states. Norman (1999) describes play as "mediator of an inner psychic world. The passions and experiences from within have no forms of their own and will use the forms in time and space in external reality" (p. 172). In describing the importance of a sense of play, Winnicott (1971) states, ". . . it is only in being creative that the individual discovers the self" (p. 54). Play implies a relationship with the other that transcends both self and other and yet, paradoxically, is the source of a sense of self. He further states, ". . . psychotherapy is done in the overlap of the two play areas, that of the patient and that of the therapist. If the therapist cannot play, then he is not suitable for the work" (p. 54).

This paradoxical idea of an evolved self able to lose one's self differs essentially from Freud's (1930a) idea of the mature ego. "Our present day ego-feeling is only a shrunken residue of a much more inclusive—indeed all-embracing—feeling which corresponded to a more intimate bond between the ego and the world about it" (Freud, 1930a, p. 68). For Freud, this relinquishment of the primitive bond characteristic of infantile mental life was the fate of the adult ego as it distinguishes the self from the external world under the influence of the reality principle (ibid., p. 67). He points out that while the mature ego has undergone development, the primitive instinctual self remains unaltered (ibid., pp. 68–69). We would have to recognise, however, that the so-called development of the mature ego might not, in fact, represent development if that instinctual self remains unaltered and undeveloped. Divided from the mature ego, both sides of the self are impoverished.

According to Bion's model of the mind and of thinking, the development of the self depends upon a *relationship* to those primitive feelings, in the process of which they can be mitigated to a certain extent by a capacity to tolerate and digest the feelings. The ego does not shrink; it is useful in facilitating the expansion of a self able to incorporate the energy of those primal states. This is Bion's (1970) definition of genius, the manipulation of primal (i.e, psychotic) thought processes in a way that promotes growth (ibid., p. 29). This primal self develops the capacity to process emotional experience, at first in relation to the mother's containing capacities that, once internalised, form the basis for the development of thought. Thinking is the outgrowth of this capacity for conscious *awareness* of those primal experiences. Along these lines, Fairbairn's (1944) structural theory takes issue with the primacy of the pleasure principle, which he sees rather as subsequent to an "impoverishment of object relations" (p. 89). It is those impoverished relationships, he says, which lead to a dependence on pleasure as a defence against the pain of early emotional deprivation in the relationship with the mother. The mother unable to provide an emotional container for primitive feelings, for instance, leaves the child with no way to process them into thought and so develop his mind.

Fairbairn also indicated that the id was included in the ego from the beginning. The ego was the *source* of impulses and tension rather than, as Freud believed, a structure that developed on the surface of the psyche to regulate id impulses (Fairbairn, 1944, p. 88). Mental health, in other words, is not a *replacement* of id by ego, as suggested by Freud's famous dictum, "Where id is, there shall ego be" (1933a, p. 80). Rather, it is characterised by a continuous dynamic *relationship* between these dual functions of the mind.

Bion's picture of a co-operative dialectical relationship between the two, an ever-shifting balance gained through the ongoing processing of primitive states, suggests that Descartes's famous dictum, "*Cogito, ergo sum*", makes more sense as "*Sum, ergo cogito*" ("I am, therefore I think"). Only if one exists, defined in the capacity to feel and process one's primitive feelings, can one think. The mind exists as a *function* of that process, so that the mind is not a thing, but an empty vessel ready to accommodate the existence of thoughts or ideas born of one's relationship to an essential metaphysical reality. From this perspective, the mind capable of emotional reality exists, at least at times, in a state of readiness to receive thoughts from a supra-human realm.

Bion (1975) used the term "binocular vision" to refer to the ability for a bi-valent focus which enables the co-operation between conscious and unconscious mental functions. "We need a kind of mental binocular vision—one eye blind [to the sensual world], the other eye with good enough sight" (Bion, 1975, p. 63). Bion amplifies this in relation to Freud's idea of consciousness.

> The use in psycho-analysis of conscious and unconscious in viewing a psycho-analytic object is analogous to the use of the two eyes in ocular observation of an object sensible to sight. Freud attributed this function, the sense organ of psychical quality, to consciousness alone. (Bion, 1962a, p. 86)

Like the relationship between these two mental functions, primitive thought processes underlying the infant's dream-like "oceanic" feeling are used in conjunction with aspects of consciousness to facilitate an experience of wholeness in the mind. In the balance of these opposing forces, the apparent loss of the ego within the oceanic waves is really the transcendence of an ego that had already been compromised (shrunken) by its unilateral focus. It represents an already pathological ego that had defensively excluded the perception of primitive modes of experience, access to which underlies the dreaming function essential to thinking, creativity, play, and passion.

Thoughts without a thinker and the self without a self

Schopenhauer wrote, "Talent . . . hits a target which others cannot reach; genius . . . hits a target which others cannot see" (Young, 2005, p. 126). This invisible or metaphysical target suggests an awareness of something new—a new thought, a creative idea—about to come into existence. It is fair to say that even the genius cannot see that target, for, until he hits it, it does not yet exist. Immersed in the *process* of creation, only that moment of creation is relevant; the *next* moment— the target or end product—has no relevance, since it does not yet exist.

Stein (1935) expressed this idea, saying, "One has no identity . . . when one is in the act of doing anything" (pp. 131–132). This reflects the suspension of ego functions in the process of being, the suspension of desire (that one might find or hit a target), and the suspension of memory (of one's past successful bulls' eyes). It is an experience of O, where what seems like a loss of self is the experience of a more essential self capable of being in the timeless primitive mind. Like the infant with virtually no experience and no means against which to judge his experience of the moment, he is less impeded in the experience of that moment. It is a *self without a self*, which cannot fully be known either by the self or the other, for it is part of an infinite whole in which *the self is a process of becoming, linked to the object or activity in an experience of at-one-ment*. To rephrase Stein's statement, we might say that, at this level of experience, one is *neither* one's self *nor* the other, *and* one is both. The self exists, in Bion's terms, in "the bit in between", an experience of non-being that is simultaneously an experience of being.

Schopenhauer's target is similar to Bion's idea of a thinker who does not create the thought; rather, the mind is activated by the need to accommodate the existence of truth. "Thinking is a function forced upon the psyche by the pressure of thoughts, not the other way around" (Bion, 1962b, p. 111). These thoughts without a thinker come unbidden from the infinite (O) to the mind of the artist or thinker. The "target" is the thought or work of art that appears in the act of creation. The sense of surprise and delight that an audience receives from a new idea or creative inspiration derives from the artist having inhabited that unknowing metaphysical mental space where the work was new and surprising to him, too.

Frost (1939) vividly describes this process of creation, "Like a piece of ice on a hot stove the poem must ride on its own melting . . . it can never lose its sense of a meaning that once unfolded by surprise as it went" (p. 178). Entering that state can be terrifying, however, as it puts the artist in touch with the dread of the "blank page", or "blank canvas", the fear of the unknown. For those who are not writers or painters this dread might be easier to visualise symbolically with reference to the strange helplessness of aiming at a target which does not exist. For the analyst, tolerating the "blank" emptiness by suspending one's ego functions helps one to hear the new and cogent thought behind the patient's plethora of associations.

The Buddhist idea of transcending one's ego by suspending rational understanding is derived through this same sense of at-one-ment with an essential reality—O. The Indian poet, Rabindranath Tagore, describes this "drunkneness" in the act of creation as the path toward union with the higher self. In the tradition of Sufism, or Persian mysticism, the oneness with the "friend", or "lord", refers to that loss of self which allows for the mystic's sense of oneness, not with a physical God, but with one's own mental experience of infinite metaphysical reality—the "God" (or O) within.

> I know that only as a singer I come before thy presence . . .
> Drunk with the joy of singing I forget myself and call thee
>   friend who art my lord."
>
> (Tagore, 1913, p. 18)

Yeats likens the innocence and simplicity in Tagore's work to the newness of the child's experience of the world, the same quality as the saints, who "seek not hidden treasures" (Yeats, (1997[1912]), p. 14). Like the "drunken" child swimming in his own oceanic feelings, these saints—or child-like mystics—do not consciously seek, and yet, in the egoless state of being/non-being, the treasures of creation find them. Like Bion's thoughts without a thinker, or Schopenhauer's invisible target, the treasure emerges from seemingly effortless non-being, since one cannot really go looking for something which does not yet exist. Not surprisingly, Picasso, whose work was a continuous and surprising chronicle of change and transformation, noted the same thing. "To search means nothing in painting. To find, that is the thing" (Flam, 1973, p. 25).

Of course, all of this is far from effortless, for it involves the disciplined preparatory work of training the mind to suspend memory, desire, and understanding as a means of entry into those primitive mental states. In these moments, the work appears to create itself, an experience aptly described by Leonard Cohen, when asked if he found it difficult to write poetry. "Poetry is just the evidence of life," he replied, "if your life is burning well, poetry is just the ash" (Cohen, 2005). The capacity to suffer the "burning"—the passion and pain of life lived with one's feelings intact—is the basis of mental integration in the mystic's relinquishment of control over one's familiar self to enter that larger experience of being. This emotional challenge and the losses of the illusion of control are compensated by those unexpected treasures, as well as the sense of an integrated self.

Being and passion: Rilke's fourth Duino elegy

Rilke's capacity to enter this selfless state in pursuit of poetry was legendary. He wrote the first two of his *Duino Elegies* in 1912, and the third and fourth within two years. For the rest, he waited ten years. And then, in what is one of the most famous feats of literary inspiration, he completed the remaining six elegies and all fifty-five of the *Sonnets to Orpheus* in just over a week. His experience was a loss of control and a loss of self, which he punctuated with screams of intense ecstasy and pain. Rilke referred to this great giving as "the most enigmatic dictation I have ever endured and achieved" (Mitchell, 2009, p. xvii).

Rilke is unmatched in his poetic descriptions of the interior landscape, and the life and death of the self. No doubt, his interest in Freud and his love affair with Lou Andreas Salomé help to inform his poems with an awareness of the parents' effects on the child's emotional development, as we see in these excerpts from the fourth Duino elegy. Rilke here addresses the child's confusing relationship with his father.

> Don't you think I'm right?
> You, father whose life tasted so bitter
> after you tasted mine
> the first thick doses of my necessity . . .
> you who loved me for my little beginning of love for you
> I always lost track of
> because the distance in your face

even as I loved it
turned into outer space
where you no longer existed . . .
(Rilke, 1912b, pp. 45–46)

Rilke gives us a clear picture of the child's exquisite sensitivity to the parents' states of mind and the awareness of their mental absence or presence. The poem continues:

> Who shows a child as he really is?
> Who sees him among the stars
> And puts the measure of distance in his hand? . . .
> . . . To contain death, the whole of death
> even before life has begun
> to contain it so gently and not to be angry -
> this is indescribable.
(Rilke, 1912b, p. 48)

Of course, the child *is* angry if he is not seen "as he really is . . . / among the stars". The child needs to be seen, that is, not only as a physical presence, but "in the stars", in his metaphysical transcendent aspects depicted in the child's intuitive awareness of his father's inner world. The parent's blindness to that profound aspect of the self leaves the child blind to himself, unable to experience his own potential for wholeness.

There is a paradox implicit in the poem, however, for, in the context of the poem, the child "among the stars" is not the same as the child in "outer space". The former represents a primal source of dreams and intuition in which the potential for wholeness resides. However, this is easily confused with the "haven" in outer space to which the child retreats to escape the pain of having a detached or absent parent, the same haven to which the child in the poem saw his father retreat. It becomes the child's prison, a retreat into unconscious hatred in which the child, like the absent father (or mother), becomes detached and unreachable. These two perspectives on emptiness and non-being are antithetical, and the inability to distinguish the two easily becomes the source of confusion that might become the compelling force in an individual's life. We see in this poem both the child's need to be seen in his original wholeness "among the stars" and the need to be seen by the parent in the divided and confused self of a state of non-being. As we shall see in the clinical examples, this is the confusion we see so often in analysis, where the patient's healthy impulse toward higher mental existence of dreams—O—is confused with the flight into a state of untethered phantasy.

The child's attempts to mask the divided self with manic or hypomanic defences designed to convince both himself and his parents that all is well is an ongoing unconscious attack on an authentic self capable of awareness, growth, and integration. The parents' unseeing eyes are experienced by the child as implicit judgements that the hidden authentic self is unwanted. It serves as further proof that his or her unheard pleas to be seen "as he really is . . . / among the stars" are dangerous and bad. According to Rilke, this living death of the self might take place "even before life has begun", although the convincing *appearance* of life is really the child's enduring mental death.

Left in an emotional vacuum, the child instead becomes a receptor for the parent's feelings. Pistiner de Cortinas (2009) writes, "Instead of the baby's primitive messages going towards the mother . . . the infant receives the undigested emotional messages from the mother . . . [which become] 'radioactive elements'" (p. 10) in the child's personality.

One anxiety-riddled patient's intense pain of having to carry his psychotic mother's insanity caused him to freeze any safe moment he was able to experience in the session in an attempt to control it and make it last forever. In the process, he strangled the pleasure of our emotional connection, along with his nascent sense of being and his sense of my existence as well. In one session, he had managed to tolerate his primitive feelings of rage long enough for him to see that both of us had survived. He had arrived at a feeling of security and gratitude. However, his fear of that one real moment of connection between us quickly caused him to freeze himself into a static state of non-being, to guard against the possibility of more dangerous rage. In safeguarding the good feeling, he had unwittingly returned to deadness, a "haven" of the familiar emotional absence in which he had spent his childhood.

With increasing knowledge of very early states of mind, we now can conjecture, as Rilke did poetically, that these traumatic events might take place at, or even before, birth. Beckett (1952) suggests this as well in *Waiting For Godot*, where he writes, "They give birth astride a grave, the light gleams an instant, then it's night once more" (p. 470).

In another short dramatic piece, Beckett (1979) wrote painfully clearly of the aetiology of this kind of early emotional trauma.

> Birth was the death of him. Again. Words are few. Dying too. Birth was the death of him. Ghastly grinning ever since. Up at the lid to come. In cradle and crib. At suck first fiasco. With the first totters. From mammy to nanny and back. All the way. Bandied back and forth. So ghastly grinning on. From funeral to funeral. To now. . . . (ibid., p. 425)

One can envision this manic "ghastly grinning" as a depiction of the infant's default persona, the manic mask behind which the real infant self withers unseen. For the child with a withdrawn mother, nursing is the first fiasco, a painful introduction to a relationship with a mother who lacks that sense of play born of a real connection.

Like Rilke, Beckett had a difficult relationship with his mother, and both creative geniuses suffered from depression and isolation. In an impossible double bind, Beckett felt shut out by an emotionally distant yet demanding mother (Bair, 1978). Rilke's mother, on the other hand, pampered him, but she lacked the ability for connection and he experienced his household as a lie. She dressed her young son in girls' clothes until he went to school, later sending him to military school, where this sensitive child felt shamed by his failure to meet the expectation to become a military man like his father (Leppman, 1984).

Beckett, the infant lost in time

I began reading Beckett's work when I was sixteen years old, for, at that time, without an analyst to illuminate some of my own primitive confusion, Beckett's writings provided a way into that primitive world with someone who apparently knew the territory. Bion once told a new patient, an actress friend of mine, that there were other paths besides analysis, that even a film might offer her a kind of interpretation (private conversation with patient, 1978). For me, Beckett's work provided some "interpretations", through the resonant states of mind of his characters, from which I could learn something of my own mind.

The characters in Beckett's great existentialist play, *Waiting For Godot* (1952), are hapless wanderers who do not know where they are, where they are going, or why. Like the infant without adequate maternal containment, they have no way to understand their own emotional reality so that they might come to understand the world outside of them. The main characters, Vladimir and Estragon, wander through this bleak landscape, fugitives from love and authentic connection, but simultaneously tortured by their inescapable needs. This is their tragic plight, caught between being and non-being, between their desires to be alive and to die. In exile from the feelings that give life a sense of meaning and reality, they seem to exist outside of time, but are repeatedly forced by their circumstances, and by each other, to come face to face with their reality. It fits the description of the insurmountable plight of the schizoid individual, who ". . . becomes subject to the compulsion to hate and be hated while all the time he longs deep down to love and to be loved" (Fairbairn, 1940, p. 26).

Vladamir and Estragon wait in this timeless universe where, paradoxically, all they have is time, by which they feel constantly tormented. They are waiting for "Godot", an unknown saviour whom they hope will deliver them from their boredom and their torturous emotional needs. In the course of this timeless, aimless journey they have a brief encounter with the slavemaster, Pozzo, and his slave, Lucky, who wander by again in the second act. By then, Pozzo and Lucky have become blind and mute, respectively. In response to being asked when the slave, Lucky, became mute, Pozzo says to Vladimir,

> "Have you not done tormenting me with your accursed time! . . . One day, is that not enough for you, one day he went dumb, one day I went blind, one day we shall die, the same day, the same second, is that not enough for you?" (Beckett, 1952, p. 470).

Implicit in this is that time itself is a torture, for to exist in time and space is to be real, a real being born into a real world of other real beings, and sometimes un-Lucky enough to experience real feelings too early and without the necessary help.

For the child in this predicament, and the one described by Rilke (above, pp. 24–25), time and reality are collapsed and almost nothing remains but an incomprehensible world of one's own imagination, bleak and lonely in its absence of attachment, meaning, and love. This collapse of time in a loveless world becomes the dominion of a terrifying superego which Bion (1970) calls the "super'ego", stripped of all the characteristics of life, a state of "non-existence" (pp. 20–21).

The child's self imposed mental exile is driven by the inability to tolerate the conflicting need and hatred for a parent emotionally incapable of helping him to bear those feelings. Hiding this hatred preserves the image of a loving parent in the child's mind, but perpetuates a false attachment (Fairbairn, 1952). Vladimir and Estragon embody this confusion between love and hate. When Estragon returns to Vladimir after a night apart, Vladimir says, "You again! Come here till I embrace you", to which Estragon replies, "Don't touch me! Don't question me! Don't speak to me! Stay with me!" (Beckett, 1952, p. 430). This ambivalence dramatises the conflict of a desperate need for a mother and the repulsion from the emotional danger of connecting with a mother who is not capable of connection. Forced to escape from objects to whom they are inexorably drawn, Beckett's characters exist in states of barely controlled despair.

The possibility of a healthy loving attachment to the mother devolves into the attachment to a cruel master/superego, played out in Lucky's savage treatment at the hands of his master, Pozzo. The ironically named slave—"Lucky"—brings attention to the pain and dread of existential freedom. While this reflects the inherent emotional challenge of having a separate autonomous self, it is often rendered impossible by an emotionally undependable parent. The loved–hated flawed parent is replaced by an omnipotent God/saviour/superego to which one is enslaved. This God that guides one's life and one's mind has the mental capacity of the infant, as yet mindless and unable to think. Mentally dead, spared the pain of reality and need, the child/slave feels himself to be "lucky", for there is no awareness of the destructive force brought to bear upon his mind, and the capacity for love that he spurns but for which he also hopelessly yearns.

Mental freedom might be experienced as chaotic or anarchic, and so one seeks to substitute the authentic container of one's own dynamic mind with enslavement to parents or internal parents, to a spouse, or an ideology, or a group, contracting the expansive mind as a way of organising it. Confined in this way, however, one may then fight off the shackles of that oppressive superego by destroying all links, thereby ending up mindless, with no container for one's feelings and thoughts. Although this gives the impression of freedom, what feels like freedom is, in fact, chaos, but there is no one mentally available to feel it. Parthenope Bion Talamo concisely underlines the distinction between the two, saying, "Liberty and anarchy are not synonymous" (Borgogno & Merciai, 2000, pp. 56–57 fn).

Kafka, of course, was also masterful at expressing this state of self-imposed exile from oneself with no knowledge of how he got there. The first line of *The Trial* reads, "Someone must have been telling lies about Joseph K., for without having done anything wrong he was arrested one morning" (Kafka, 1937, p. 1). The internal prison, meant to isolate the feeling self from the pain of needing an absent object, is a lie of the mind that erodes its capacity as a vessel for truth.

It might seem disrespectful or reductionistic to describe these great works of art in terms of pathology, but, for me, it is based on an appreciation of the endurance of the essential self still able to express itself despite these ancient defences. It is also a recognition that creativity and pathology derive from the same source—the primitive experiences of the child. The survival and health of the essential infant self depends upon the invention of ways to transform its experiences into dreams and other expressions of the incarceration of the self. In Cocteau's words, scribbled on a drawing at an exhibition of his work, "The artist is a prison from which the work of art escapes" (Cocteau, 1993).

Clinical example

I will end this chapter with a clinical example that addresses the experiences of life and death in the mind.

"Giselle"

"Giselle" is a bright young woman whose mother was schizophrenic. Despite feelings of crushing insecurity regarding her work and her relationships, she has managed to become a successful lawyer, although she is frequently drawn back into phantasies of a perfect womb-mother who will fix all her problems. Terrified by her own development, she often mistrusts me, while at other times she challenges her deadening escapes from feeling and from reality, fiercely defending her analysis and almost never missing a session. At the time of this session, a move to a new home aroused feelings of anxiety, abandonment, loss, dread, and confusion.

I dreamt I found a new house [in reality she was still looking] but it wasn't so beautiful. I felt anxious about moving and a friend said, "Minds heal, but slowly . . . you're anxious." I said to her, "Don't tell me how I feel!" She suggested I listen to some New Age music, which I hate, and I was annoyed. I then went to a café and ordered coffee, half regular and half decaf. The woman working there annoyed me because she was so slow, although she was being very nice.

Giselle spoke of how anxious she feels, she likes her current home and does not want to move, but her work demands it. She had had a thought the day before that she would be able to find a place eventually, but that it was slow. She described her friend in the dream as someone she loves, who had, in fact, played some music for her by an *avant garde* singer. Unlike her friend, Giselle does not like that music. She added that she does drink her coffee with half decaf, and she felt impatient in the dream because the woman had to brew it specially for her, heat the water and grind the beans, and "it just took too long".

I thought that I was probably Giselle's friend whom she "loves", and yet does not like me to talk about what she feels. Perhaps more to the point, however, I thought that it was her internal "friend", a voice of reason with whom she intermittently has contact, but at the moment she does not want to "move" and so has no interest in hearing the truth from either of us. Her anxiety reflects her feelings about the birth of her mind and self—her feeling *and* reason—as she leaves her old home of her mother's womb, offering her a retreat into the unconsciousness of her ideal phantasy. She likes it there and, on the one hand, wants no part of this difficult challenge of having a mind.

I said that I thought I was the annoying woman in the café, who takes so long to help her, while her old phantasy seems able to fix her immediately by killing off any painful feelings of vulnerability and need. Unfortunately, this is an illusion and she remains stuck there in the same mindlessness. She would like me to stop thinking as well, stop grinding my analytic "bean", stop letting her music brew in my mind as I make an interpretation especially for her. Like the caffeine, this might wake her up, so she would prefer me to be like her internal mother, who does not listen to or communicate with her, and does not think. Her "new house" would include a mind able to think and feel, which does not look as beautiful as her illusory phantasy of perfection.

In short, Giselle is stuck between her desire for being and non-being. I pointed out this dilemma, for, as we see, she wants "half decaf, half regular" coffee, hoping that she can be half awake while remaining half asleep, hoping to be born just halfway. Nonetheless, it was important to recognise her desire to change which, while reluctant, she expressed at the beginning of the session, "I don't want to move *but I have to . . . for work.*" There is a sense here that her desire for stasis and non-existence is a ship that has sailed, that despite her terror and her desire to remain in a foetal state, she is impelled by, and already into, the process of being born.

CHAPTER THREE

The development of language

"We often talk in a way which sounds exactly as if we talked the same language. It is very doubtful"

(Bion, 1975, p. 23)

"We speak of things we do not know
knowing we will never know
though in the effort we are human—
whatever that is"

(Reiner, 2010b)

P sychoanalysis presents many challenges for analyst and analysand alike. Not the least of these is the paradox at its core, since analysis relies largely on verbal language to examine an essentially non-verbal world, the non-sensual, infinite realm of the mind, of dreams and unconscious mental energies, which defies verbal description. In addition, like the inhabitants of Babel, humanity is cursed by a profusion of tongues that amount to much more than the approximately 6,700 worldwide languages. Because each mind is different in infinitely complex ways, we are dealing with a vastly greater number of ways of using language in each person's idiosyncratic mode of thinking. There is no single language for the unconscious; even in one person, the vocabulary of dreams changes from day to day, and in the conversations and relationships between internal objects, each individual mind speaks in multitudinous languages of its own. From this opulence of meaning and meaninglessness, the analyst and analysand are called upon together to forge a living language in which to communicate these enigmatic states of mind.

Bion (1992) often addressed the challenges related to communication. "The language of ordinary human beings is only appropriate to the rational, can only describe the rational, can only make statements in terms of rationality" (p. 371). Clinical observations reveal to us that problems in communication and language are inextricably linked to problems in thinking, and so the importance of language as an instrument of mental development, a means for higher conceptual thinking, compels the analyst to address this challenge. In this chapter, we will examine the development of language and the obstacles to its development, as well as some of its precursors in primitive states of mind.

Language and primitive mental states

Since we use verbal language in our efforts to communicate with pre-verbal, infantile aspects of our patients, the question arises as to whether pre-verbal infants "understand" language, and if so, how. These are questions that can be explored but not definitively answered, although increases in our knowledge of pre-natal life and the psychoanalytic inferences drawn from it have by now provided more information from which to conjecture.

Implicit in Norman's (2004) psychoanalytic work with infants is the idea that some kind of meaningful communication is possible, even with pre-verbal babies. He observed that infants read facial expressions and "understand emotional meaning when there is a concordance between the lexical [verbal] and non-lexical [sounds, intonations, gestures] aspects of the spoken language" (2004, p. 1106). Although Norman found no evidence that the infant could understand the lexical aspects of language, he did think that the infant was "able to process certain aspects of language" (Norman, 2001, p. 5). On

the faces of even the youngest infants, we can observe their rapt attention and intense curiosity when being spoken to, especially if one
communicates something meaningful to them on an emotional level.
Norman (2001) notes that when the lexical meaning is in tune with the
non-lexical aspects, tone of voice, facial expression, etc., infants will
pay more attention. So, while we assume that they cannot possibly
understand the words or content of what is being said, there is a form
of understanding related more to the music and the speaker's understanding than to the meaning of the words themselves.

My own clinical experience with a mother and infant in treatment
(Reiner, 2010a) led me to think that while babies cannot *understand* the
words, they seem to *gain understanding* from the analyst's verbal
communications. It is a more passive and primitive form of mental
processing which seems related to projective identification, although,
in this case, the infant identifies with the *mental function* of understanding, with the mother's or adult's capacity for alpha function.

Bion's notion of a pre-conception describes a kind of mental aspect
of an instinct. This pre-conception is a state of expectation, a readiness
to meet with an inherent instinctual need, like the infant's expectation
of a nipple to fill its empty mouth and, perhaps or, an expectation of
food/milk to fill its empty stomach. "The mating of pre-conception
and realization brings into being the conception" (Bion, 1963, p. 23).
Given Bion's idea of thinking as an instinctual need, we would have
to consider thinking itself as an innate preconception. We might see it
as a preconception of the existence of thoughts potentially able to fill
the empty space of a mind instinctually programmed to think, a preliminary or proto-capacity to think about the sensations, experience,
feelings, etc., which make up one's inner life. Related to O as a representation of a primal proto-mental knowledge, it is an as yet unillu-
minated capacity, the inherent potential for truth, thinking, and
higher consciousness waiting to be fulfilled. As I described elsewhere:

> Since [thinking] is part of the as yet undeveloped psycho-physical
> potential to which each infant is attuned and toward which each is
> driven, I suggest that it is this which the infant recognizes in someone
> who speaks to his or her emotional experience in a mindful and mean-
> ingful way. This pre-conception of his own potential for thought and
> language allows him to sense in meaningful verbal communication a
> psycho-biological inheritance held for him in trust, as it were, in a kind

of 'memory of the future,' as he is driven to develop that potential. (Reiner, 2010a, p. 158)

A study by Condon and Sander (1974) testing neonatal responses to speech found that, as early as the first day of life, infants showed organised rhythmic bodily responses to adult speech patterns of meaningful language. This capacity for what they called "interactional synchrony" was seen to indicate that the form and structure of language is laid down in the body long before one learns to speak. We might think about the pre-verbal child's mysterious capacity to understand something of verbal language as similar to the capacity to find meaning in music or poetry. Even if one cannot rationally understand it, a poem might make a certain kind of sense to the reader, touching something beyond language that can reintroduce the reader to a part of himself with which he might have temporarily lost contact.

Language and individuation

Language implies the existence of separateness from other individuals with whom one needs a way to communicate. Language itself, based on separateness, might, therefore, be experienced as a disturbance to the infantile phantasy of fusion with the mother. This presents an obstacle with critical implications for clinical work, for it means that the analyst's very use of language might itself be experienced as a threat to that primal phantasy, an impingement on a foetal state of mind *no matter what the content* of the interpretation. In dealing with some patients at a primitive pre-verbal, even pre-natal level, defences against this threat might render the interpretations incomprehensible, obviously an essential impediment in a "talking cure" (Freud, 1895d). At this level, even the neurotic patient might experience words as physical attacks. For one patient who was sexually abused, for instance, any contact felt like a dangerous intrusion into her carefully constructed fortress against the confusion and pain of rape, and she began to feel my words as penetrating her anus or vagina, naturally leading her fiercely to reject them. Clearly, these confusions about language itself need to be interpreted before any meaningful communication can take place in the analysis.

Freud's discussion of his small grandson's "Fort–Da" game (1920g) makes the connection between the child's first words and his attempts to deal with separation from mother. As touched upon earlier (above, p. 11), Bion's (1970) idea of the "no-thing" also relates the origin of thought, and so also of language, to the capacity for awareness of the mother's absence. The development of thinking is dependent on the capacity to tolerate the attendant feelings of need in order to experience a space in the mind for the thought, "no-mother" or "no-breast", to exist. Lacan also points out that the mother's act of naming represents a differentiation of mother and child. He calls language "the murder of the thing", where the absence of the object stimulates the mind with a desire to substitute a word for the missing thing (Muller & Richardson, 1982, pp. 400–402). Lacan's choice of words suggests something of the emotional violence associated with the development of language as an outgrowth of feelings of separateness.

Pre-natal knowledge

Bion's concept of O presumes a kind of truth known to us on an instinctual level beyond conscious awareness. Plato's idea of pure Forms also describes the existence of an innate non-empirical knowledge, where learning is a recollection of a now forgotten knowledge known to us before birth. Plato (360 BC) writes,

> [If] the knowledge we acquired before birth was lost by us at birth, and if afterwards by the use of the senses we recovered what we previously knew, will not the process which we call learning be a recovering of the knowledge that is natural to us, and may not this be rightly termed recollection? (p. 108)

One is remembering, in other words, one's own forgotten knowledge. The following poem expresses something of this process.

The Naked I

> Take off your dark glasses
> take off your mother's glasses, your father's glasses,
> your blind theories of everything you know -
> better yet, take off your clothes.
> From bare trees green leaves will fall into your hand

and you will read them like a gypsy with crystal vision.
All over town you'll see nothing but naked children—
bankers, lawyers, doctors
who otherwise appear so permanently dressed—
will show you their soft bellies and secret scars.
Teachers strip curricula
and instruct children only to keep their eyes naked,
to see for the first time
what they've always known.

                                                      (Reiner, 1994)

Bion (1977a) conjectured about this level of primal knowledge, remnants of a pre-natal experience stored in forgotten areas of the mind–body. These "proto-mental" vestiges of experience are seen to be unretrievable to explicit memory. Mancia (2006) points out that the mother's speech is stored in implicit memory, and has emotional significance to the infant and prenate before it has semantic significance. These primal memories differ from Freud's idea of a repressed memory, for never having been represented mentally they cannot be repressed and so they inhabit a sort of non-existent desert of the mind incapable of being remembered. They can, however, be experienced in the transference where, according to Mancia (2006), they can be emotionally or experientially "remembered" and so thinkable, though still not remembered in their original form. What is remembered might be loosely compared to an artist's print transferred on to paper from a woodblock or etching, where the original image—like the primal past—is visible only as an imprint.

Neuroscientist Regina Pally describes "implicit memory" as the infant's most primal pre-verbal reminiscences. Even *in utero*, the foetus can recognise the mother's voice, so that

> ... certain information can be stored in memory without our having been consciously aware of its occurrence ... implicit memory includes the memory of shape and form ... emotion ... and skills, habits and routines (procedural memory), each of which is processed in a different brain system (Pally, 1997, par. 23)

Implicit memory, mediated by sub-cortical regions of the brain, which regulate functions of the amygdala concerned with emotion, is similar to what Bion described as proto-mental experiences.

Rilke's Ninth Elegy

This excerpt from Rilke's ninth *Duino Elegy* considers the role of language in expressing the essential nature of things and of the self, a celebration and appreciation of existence itself. While human beings shrink from life knowing they will die, at the same time they yearn to be part of life, "just because to be here means so much . . ." (Rilke, 1912b, p. 77).

> Are we on this earth only to say: *house,*
> *bridge, fountain, gate, jug, fruit tree, window*—
> at best:
> *column . . . tower?*
> But to say these words, you understand,
> with an intensity
> the things themselves
> never dreamed they'd express . . ..
> *Here* is the time for the unsayable . . .
> Speak, bear witness.
> More than ever things fall away from us
> liveable things
> and what crowds them out and replaces them
> is an event for which there is no image.
>
> (Rilke, 1912b, pp. 80–81)

We are compelled to speak by virtue of being alive, both physically and mentally. As Bion (1975) put it, if we have minds, ". . . we shall have to do something about them" (p. 50). To begin with, our instinctual heritage impels us to develop these minds, to fulfil an inherent potential to organise numinous experience into images and thinkable forms such as language. Rilke addresses the struggle to communicate something of this numinous thing-in-itself, the need to express this mysterious hidden realm. The idea of "liveable things" which are crowded out and replaced seems to refer to the frustrations of a mind which is not sufficiently alive to one's own hidden experiences to be able to think them, "events for which there is no image". On the one hand, one is also up against the natural limitations of having to rely on finite minds to encompass an infinite world, but with those "liveable" experiences crowded out through pathological defences which separate one from one's emotional life, one's capacity to think is obstructed.

In the extract below, Rumi also describes the responsibility to try to express the "unsayable", the mysterious truths, for, despite the limitations of language, it is the best method available to help potentiate the capacities for truth and higher thinking which are instrumental in integrating and making sense of our experiences.

> There is a sea that is not far from us.
> It is unseen but it is not hidden,
> It is forbidden to talk about
> Yet at the same time
> It is a sin and a sign of ungratefulness
> Not to.
>
> Rumi (1993a, p. 15)

Hearing the music of the session

This next clinical example focuses on the need to hear the silent communications in the session, so that we may try to speak for the patient some of these unsayable things.

"Helen": Session 1

"Helen" is a bright, curious woman in her fifties who is devoted to analysis and to her own growth and "enlightenment". She had a traumatic childhood, beginning with a premature birth and parents who exerted little control over her violent brother, who often preyed on this sensitive little girl. Her means of survival in this chaotic family was to lose herself in the creative gifts of an innately active imagination. Steeling herself against the continuing abuse and disappointment, she created a world apart, isolated and detached. After many years of analysis, she has developed her talents as a painter and an art teacher, and has become painfully aware of her difficulties in relationships. She feels tormented by the primitive feelings of need and separateness from which she so long ago detached herself. The anxiety and despair that have emerged with the psychic birth of that buried self have played out in the transference in painful ways for us both. Her resistance to contact with an authentic self, and with me, was, for many years, fierce. This session affords us a view of the subtleties in "hearing" those inaudible, non-verbal aspects of the patient's communication which obstruct contact with truth and authentic feeling—with O.

Helen was animated as she reported all the good things happening with her work. As I listened, I grew increasingly uncomfortable, without knowing exactly why. I wondered why I felt annoyed, even angry at times, in view of the positive content. Helen went on to describe having helped one of her art students work on a painting whose theme he characterised as "reckless and out of control". Helen felt pleased to have been able to help the man communicate this through what she called the "music" of the painting—its form and movement, rather than only through its subject matter. I then said that I was thinking about what music she was expressing in the story she was telling me. She became irritated with me and said, "Just let me tell you what happened!" I said, "I had a thought about the theme *you* might be expressing and thought I would share it with you, but apparently you'd prefer not to hear from me today." Again, she replied angrily, "Can I just finish what I was saying!?"

I said that she was free to say whatever she wished, but she did not seem to accord me the same freedom. The intensity of Helen's anger helped me to realise that the irritation I felt earlier was due to her underlying hostility to "us" as a working analytic couple, for she was here the teacher–analyst–mother who could help herself and did not need my, or anyone's, help. It was a re-enactment of that old story, for she seemed to be "teaching" me about things she already knew, things which had happened "yesterday", that is, in the past, in order to avoid the reality of what was actually happening between us in the present moment. She was avoiding, that is, her need to learn, her need for me to *help* her learn, avoiding the unknown truth (O) of our moment together. Her enactment of these past defences were, in fact, all happening in the past, and on that level she had no experience of me or of herself in the room. My attempts at interpretation had been an annoying intrusion into her phantasy.

While this is a common occurrence in analysis, it is tricky, for such an obstruction of reality, of O, of the patient's own sense of being and being present, can only be heard—or really felt—if the analyst is authentically experiencing what is going on in herself or himself, and what is going on in the room. My annoyance was not only due to the projection of her anger, but also to feeling devalued and dismissed, having the truth dismissed in favour of phantasies. These are feelings she no doubt felt all her life. The interpretations I made were valid only in *this particular relationship with Helen in this particular moment*. I could, therefore, communicate to her a sense of her intention to obstruct her own existence, but, despite my attempts to write about it here, it cannot really be adequately communicated to anyone who was not there.

What I pointed out to Helen was that while she was going over the things she already understood, there was something happening in addition to that right now which I had thought she might be interested to know about. Apparently, I had been wrong. Helen was silent and appeared to be listening to me. I went on to say that while I could really appreciate her being pleased with her work, I had also heard something else in the "music" of her words, more along the lines of feeling "reckless and out of control" inside, and that seemed related to her feelings in *our* work. She became annoyed again, but after a moment told me that she had awakened this morning feeling unbearably lonely.

I suggested that if, as I thought, she did not want to hear what I said and I was not allowed to speak with her or really be present, she was naturally feeling very lonely, apparently without even knowing it, for mentally she was, in fact, alone. She said, "I felt that all the time as a child, my mother wasn't aware of my existence." Like Rilke's awareness of his father's emotional absence (above, pp. 24–25), Helen sensed her mother's lack of emotional presence, which meant that Helen felt unseen and absent as well. In the transference, I had become her unreasonable mother whom she felt never listened to her feelings, but in her complex and confused object relations, it was she who had become her absent mother, unaware of my existence and her own.

From the perspective of this idealised mother, I was her student/baby self she could help. I, her analyst, was irrelevant. Having no need of me, Helen had put me in a box, unconsciously communicating to me what she had done to herself, and how angry, terrified, and lonely it made her. My actual presence as her analyst was unwanted evidence of a painful outside world. For a brief moment, however, this frustrated and angry baby was able to tolerate my presence and hear me. Helen then said she felt frightened; she started to cry. Again, something did not ring true. I felt manipulated and, once more relying on her non-verbal communications, I felt as if she were trying to invoke my feelings of pity, which I did not feel. I felt she was keeping me out, and keeping out her feelings, an intention beneath her tears that, to my ear, struck a very different chord than genuine fear or loneliness.

I told Helen that I thought she was feeling afraid to feel anything, that she was frustrated and angry and wanted me to take pity on her and stop talking. She took a deep breath, and through tears which now *did* feel genuine, she said, "I feel my loneliness like a bone-eating cancer . . . (Pause) . . . No, I don't want to listen to you." I could feel in *my* bones the kind of morbid toxic feeling she had described, a poison that was directed toward her feelings and toward me, and toward us as an analytic couple. She said that she wanted to die and did not care about herself, to which I added that she wanted me dead as well so that she could stay dead. She said, "I want everyone dead." I pointed out that this was how she felt with her family as she escaped into her imagination—a temporary refuge against her confused rage. Helen was silent for several minutes. She then said, "I just had an image of an impenetrable wall . . . I don't know how to get through it."

This wall behind which Helen had locked herself was both the product and the source of her searing and enduring loneliness. While she felt terrified and hopeless, I now felt she was in the room with me and I had a real relationship with a very scared, sad, and confused baby, as well as a very scared, sad, and confused grown-up. This was quite a different story from her superficially cheerful tone at the beginning of the session, the underlying music of which had been so grating to me.

The key to hearing this inaudible music was in my feelings of anger and loneliness, in Helen's efforts to silence me and make me a lonely and useless analyst (mother) without a patient (or child). She, thereby, ensures the continuation of her unending hopelessness and loneliness. I had a sense now of a real person, and the sense of passion between us as separate people was evident in the *com*passion I could now feel for her in contrast to my earlier irritation. Although she was distraught to feel trapped in her loneliness, she now *knew* she was trapped and lonely, which, at this moment, was the truth of her authentic being, which she was sharing with me. She had allowed herself contact with O—the emerging truth of the lonely wall she had unconsciously erected around herself so long ago.

CHAPTER FOUR

"A rose is a rose is a rose . . .": the power and limits of language

"One difficulty . . . concerns the communication of material from an experience that is ineffable; the scientific approach, as ordinarily understood, is not available and an aesthetic approach requires an artist"

(Bion, 1965, p. 51)

"In psycho-analysis we have to manufacture our means of communicating while we are communicating"

(Bion, 1975, p. 31)

B ecause the analyst uses common everyday language based on the physical world of phenomena to describe the metaphysical realities of the mind, it might seem to the patient that he and the analyst are engaged in a "normal" conversation. It often takes quite a while for the patient to become aware that the analyst is actually speaking a different language.

These challenges of language were an important topic in Bion's later work. After hearing a session described in supervision and clinical seminars, Bion often asked, "What language is this patient speaking?" (Bion, 1977b). Like a Zen *koan*, the meaning of this question was enigmatic, and, since the patient being discussed was quite obviously speaking English, the group was inevitably stumped. We were forced to consult with a non-linear, non-rational part of our minds, the result of which was more questions. For one thing, to what kind of language was Bion referring, and what kind of language was Bion speaking?

My own clinical experience eventually revealed, as we saw in Helen's session in the previous chapter, that at times the patient might not be speaking at all, at least if we view language as a means of communication between two people aware of each other's presence. Instead, the patient is speaking to an internal object, making the analyst either non-existent or a shadow of the patient's inner world. Since language capable of bridging the gap between two people with unique and separate minds reflects the developmental capacity for individuation, the patient lacking this capacity is unaware that he or she is speaking to a separate individual outside the self.

As Bion (1975) often remarked, human beings are "clever monkeys" (p. 55), capable of impressive acts of mimicry, both physical and mental. Even at early levels of development, almost everyone easily learns the language of his or her culture, but detecting the difference between imitative speech which *sounds like* practicable language and that which *actually* communicates is another matter (Paul, 1997). It is the difference between a language that emanates from a true emotional self and a language whose aim is to hide the truth of the inner world, even from oneself.

Metaphor and the language of the unconscious

Bion's (1992) idea that ordinary language is only "appropriate to the rational" (p. 371) poses a linguistic challenge. We can see roots to this in neurological development. Nobel prize winning biologist and neuroscientist Gerald Edelman (2006) writes, "Brains operate primarily not by logic but rather by pattern recognition . . . it is likely that early human thought proceeded by metaphor . . . The metaphorical capacity of linking disparate entities derives from the [mind's] associative properties . . ." (pp. 57–58). Lakoff and Johnson's (2003) study of linguistics describes metaphorical thought as mostly unconscious and related to pre-verbal structure.

To meet the patient in that metaphysical realm of O beyond the senses, the analyst relies on the same tools as the poet—metaphors, similes, symbols—which link external images to internal experience in an effort to communicate verbally something of a hidden, non-verbal world. However, while these tools allow us to communicate aspects of the mysteries of the mind, the world of symbol and metaphor is itself a mysterious language which some patients might not yet speak, not yet having developed the capacity to symbolise. Because analysis deals with these primitive precursors of thought, the analyst must first help the patient to develop a mind capable of understanding symbolic language. This mind capable of *relationships* between words and ideas is first of all based on the *relationships* between people, and so it is by addressing these fundamental issues in the transference that meaningful communication begins to become possible.

The images of a metaphor or simile are ephemeral, for they straddle metaphysical and physical reality, or inner and outer reality. Like the poet, the analyst finds himself engaged in a struggle to express that which is written between the lines. In part, this is what gives poetry its evanescent quality. The images of a metaphor, for instance, a sunny afternoon ". . . ready to burst like a ripe orange" (Valery, 1950, p. 77), or a simile, "the soft pudding of my face" (Schwartz, 1954, p. 147), derive their substance and meaning from *the relationship between the two images* compared. It is in the interstices of this intangible lexical relationship that mental reality exists.

The relationship between people functions in a similar way, an idea that Bion (1975) underlined often. "Speaking psychoanalytically, what we are concerned with is the relationship, not the things related" (p. 33). Meaning exists, in other words, in "the bit in between". Like the two sides of a metaphor, the analyst and analysand derive their meaning in that moment from the contact between them, in the empty space metaphorically suggested by Bion's use of the symbol O. It is far more complex, of course, than even this condensed extended metaphor, which Rilke wrote as his epitaph.

> Rose, pure contradiction, joy
> to be nobody's sleep under that many
> eyelids.
>
> (Leppman, 1984, p. 381)

It requires a kind of waking trance to dream the spaces in which images such as these give meaning to each other, and to us.

Intersubjectivity reflects a similarly intangible link between the two fields of interacting energies between patient and analyst. The ephemeral reality created in that intersubjective process evokes the image of a neutrino, a sub-atomic particle like an electron, but with no electric charge and almost no mass (Asimov, 1966). Travelling at the speed of light, this fundamental but elusive sub-atomic particle, like the mind itself, can only be apperceived by indirect means. Neutrinos have very little energy on their own, but while they were at first thought to be pure mythology, these "ghost particles" or "nothing particles" turned out to be real (ibid., p. xii). Analysts are up against a realm of similarly dubious existence, without the means to measure, in any sensually observable way, the intense but unseen thoughts, impressions, and emotional sensations that take place between two minds. Nonetheless, at the deepest level of the self the heat created in the space between people can provide energy that gives meaning and passion to human experience. These ideas about the sub-atomic world are themselves metaphorical rather than scientific, for there is no evidence of what, if any, correlations exist between the deepest unseen energies of internal and external existence.

Clinical example: "Dr M"

The following clinical example illustrates the misleading uses of language to which primitive states can give rise. We can see something here of the kind of communication which does not depend upon the words but on the developmental level of the person speaking.

"Dr M" is a professor and clinical psychologist in analysis for seven years. He is co-operative, but seems sometimes not to be able to use what he learns in our sessions. He was brought up by a mother addicted to amphetamines, who had a psychotic break. Sensitive and intelligent, he is devoted to his work, although, on a primitive level, his work as a psychologist still carries his phantasied wish to cure his sick mother. He oscillates between these feelings of power, and the helplessness and terror of that little unloved and unseen baby.

In this session, he described having mixed up an appointment with Dr X, a respected mentor whom he had hoped could help him implement changes in the educational system for psychologists. The patient felt bad about missing the appointment, but said, "It's not so bad, I wasn't beating myself up for my mistake like I usually do. I didn't expect myself to be perfect this time." As I listened, I sensed something lurking beneath his words. I felt, in fact, that he was engaged in that same familiar battle, a full-scale internal trial in which he was defendant, prosecutor, and defence attorney. How one senses this is mysterious and intangible, but there was something false in his tone. Not having further evidence, I waited. He told me his dream.

> I was admiring a colleague's new phone, but then it expanded to the size of an iPad and I thought, "It's too big, it's cumbersome, I'm OK with my old phone." ... Then I was explaining my ideas to Dr X about a new educational system, and I started wondering, "Why am I telling him all this, he's not interested." But I thought maybe it was good to talk anyway, just to articulate my thoughts.

Dr M said he had considered getting an iPhone but found it complicated and hard to use. He again mentioned that Dr X was perfectly understanding about the missed appointment, and they had rescheduled. The conversation with Dr X in the dream reminded the patient of having met another colleague at a conference who had in reality seemed interested in his ideas. However, Dr M then recalled having felt out of sorts that day, and he was now thinking that the colleague might have noticed this and thought ill of him.

The dream and associations seemed to confirm my sense early in the session of some other more subtle primitive feelings of which Dr M was unaware, a feeling of being judged. I interpreted that while he is professionally committed to implementing change in the educational system, he is far less committed to changes to his internal system of education, for he still prefers his "old phone", lost in a conversation with judgemental internal objects. From this perspective, he not only missed the appointment with Dr X, but, metaphorically, he is missing his session with me as well. Since he comes to see me every day, he seems to want to hear what I have to say, but anything other than that familiar internal system feels to him like the new iPhone/iPad, "too big, cumbersome and hard to use". Despite the pain it causes him, the constant cruel judgements, he keeps deciding that he is "OK with his old phone", preferring the familiarity of this ongoing internal trial to having an actual conversation with me. After hearing this interpretation, Dr M felt very sad, because he wants my help, but he was also enraged to be confronted with his dilemma. After a silence, he said, "I feel terrified . . . if I change he won't know who I am." Learning to use his new "big" phone would mean that his mind would also have to grow bigger, he would have to leave the enwombed fortress which feels safe, but deprives him of a real self capable of development.

Dr M began to breathe heavily. As I listened to his breathing, it seemed neither like anxiety nor relief, nor any other deep feeling. It felt rather like a communication for which he had no words. I began to experience his deep exhales as a means of trying to rid himself of what I had said and the feelings it aroused, as if expelling these dangerous ideas through his breath. I recognised it as another version of his long time habit of blowing his nose after an interpretation, which served the same primitive purpose, as if his feelings and my words *about* those feelings were mucous he could toss in the waste-basket. The "music" of his communication today was more complex, however, for his sighing was so exaggerated that I also felt in it a plea for me to hear how much he was suffering and come to his rescue by taking back what I had said. This "phone call" from me felt too big, and he wanted me to save him magically, as he had "saved" his mother, to avoid the awareness that might eventually lead to real change. I suppose I was meant to feel guilty, which led me to think that he could not bear the guilt of wanting to change while also aware of acting against those desires, an act against himself and me.

This was played out in the sessions that followed, in which Dr M clearly expressed his desire for me *to tell him lies*, as he was used to doing for himself. He wanted me to make him feel better at any cost, and he admitted he had no objection to my wasting his time, his money, and his life in order to re-establish his illusions. As in my experience with Helen, these intuitions about Dr M's behaviour were in part made possible by having noticed my own lack of empathy for his melodramatic sighs, or for Helen's "crocodile tears".

There is some truth to Dr M's assessment of himself as a rebel and a free thinker, trying to bring change and enlightenment to the institution in which he teaches, and to his life. He is, in fact, extremely intuitive and, at times, courageous in speaking the truth in his work situations. However, as we see here, he continues to undermine his own efforts, for, at a primitive level, he is more devoted to stasis than to change. It was devastating for him to recognise this ongoing sabo-tage in both his internal and external life. From this perspective, I am not the only one felt to be the disinterested Dr X/mother, for inter-nally, Dr M is also disinterested in hearing his own plans to change the internal system. While he can hear and often seem moved by my interpretations, he often dismisses them after the session. This session helped to shed some light on the obstruction in our work, which we can now more directly address.

In this clinical example, what language was Dr M speaking? Was it the language of a baby? A foetus? And what language does one speak to a foetus? He tells himself in the dream that it does not really matter if anyone is listening, so while it sounds as if he is talking *to* *me*, at times he is just talking, and no one, internally or externally, is felt to be listening. Like his heavy breaths, it is hot air. In the process, he negates my existence, as well as his own, for the passion which Bion described as evidence of two people present in the session is missing. There is just him, and, of course, the characters of his inter-nal world.

On one level, Dr M is in a phantasy of being in a cloistered womb, neither speaking to me nor even in the same room or the same decade with me, but, on another level, he clearly knows that he is in the present, in my consulting room. The foetal Dr M distrusts me as some-one come to destroy his detachment and numbness. But, of course, it is not only me he distrusts. It was evident to both of us that his words of change did not match their presumed intention, and so he finds, painfully, that he cannot trust himself either. His own mind, thus, provides him no reliable gauge of his beliefs or his values, leaving him in a state of confusion. As he becomes increasingly aware of this dilemma, it also becomes clear that this highly intelligent and accom-plished man does not speak a language he himself can understand.

Words spoken at this primitive level sound like words but lack the power and meaning of words that aid in thinking or communicating. They are not products of the mind (alpha elements), but felt rather to be like mucous or tears or other bodily excretions, even the hot empty air of a heavy sigh. These bits of undigested experiences (beta ele-ments) inapplicable for use in thinking (Bion, 1962a, 1963, 1970), can be projected destructively, like ammunition, or, as we saw in these examples, used to communicate non-verbal or pre-verbal experiences. These ersatz words have often been sexualised, as we saw with the

sexually molested patient who experienced interpretations as penetrating her vagina or anus (above p. 36).

The significance of Bion's enigmatic question becomes clear, for, as
we see in these cases, the kind of language the patient is speaking
becomes a matter of great consequence. It provides necessary information about the obstructions to the patient's mental development,
which must be addressed in order to develop a foundation for
communication.

The language of the arts

Awareness of these obstacles, as well as the need to create a new kind
of *ad hoc* language designed for the moment at hand, makes it more
clear why analytic discourse is such a daunting task. It is as if a painter
had first to invent paint in order to do his work. In a way, this is true
in the aesthetic world as well, especially in modern and contemporary
art, which has historically required the creation of new visual languages, new forms capable of expressing a new cultural *zeitgeist*. These
new visual forms provide fresh ways to expand past the existing hori-
zons into changing realms of emotional and social reality. The visual
languages of Impressionist art, for instance, capable of effectively
communicating the cultural reality of its time, may no longer express
a more current perspective as these paintings, once revolutionary and
shocking, become acceptable "decor" in every home and building.
While the original masterpieces retain their freshness and beauty, the
repetitions of old forms, once born of the transformations in O, begin
to bear the deadening stamp of the familiar. Like so much visual
Muzak, they lack the emotional power to represent more urgent cultural messages, becoming invisible to that deeper self whose development is dependent on new truths.

A rose is (not necessarily) a rose . . .

"A rose is a rose is a rose . . ."—at least if we interpret Gertrude Stein's
(1913, p. 178) statement as a reference to an essential nature, the rose
as thing-in-itself (O). However, the same is not true of the word
"rose", which may have different idiosyncratic meanings for each

person. Words, especially nouns that represent physical objects, are often taken at face value in everyday discourse, for they have meanings seemingly more easily agreed upon. However, even these carry imprints of the personality that impose idiosyncratic meaning. If one listens intuitively, one can hear in someone's speech a blueprint of the emotional world, although it is often unclear what one is hearing. In the internal world of symbol and metaphor, therefore, a rose is not necessarily a rose, just as a madeleine is not necessarily the madeleine Proust had in mind. It is even more complicated when the word represents a concept like "love" or "truth" or "god", rather than a concrete and visible object, what seems linguistically straightforward might mask vast discrepancies in meaning, leading to immense confusion in communication. Abused patients' confusion about what their parents mean by "I love you" is a common example, for it could mean, "I hate you", "Don't leave me", etc. The individual himself might ascribe to his words "common" usage when, in fact, they carry other, often primitive meanings, making it difficult to differentiate between words which communicate and words which sound like communication but whose aim is to obstruct communication.

The language of the mystic and the language of nonsense

Artistic movements such as Dada have arisen out of the awareness of these incongruities of words which fail accurately to communicate mental life. Dada was an art of sense and nonsense, an expression of a primitive unconscious as well as the highest aspirations of man. Jean Arp, the modernist writer, artist, and father of the Dada movement, said that as a young boy he drew pictures of "unknown dream places . . . It was in dreams that I learned how to write" (Jean, 1974, p. xv). He was thought to be distracted and inattentive in his class on religion until the priest discovered he was drawing beautiful scenes from religious history, after which young Jean was recognised as being a special student (ibid., p. xv).

Like Bion, Arp saw dreams as the primitive birthplace of timeless truth. The Dadaist aim of modern artistic expression was to keep this dream-like visual knowledge alive as a way of reflecting man's relationship to the infinite rather than to the ephemera of civilisation. Arp called the latter, "the terrifying, the threatening, the horrible, the noisy aspects of our modern machine-world . . . the curtain concealing the true mise-en-scene of the eternal spectacle" (Jean, 1974, p. 311). Art, as he saw it, was to "advanc[e] toward the absolute" (ibid., p. 315).

The often primitive use of language in Dada writings reflects the idea of intellect as secondary in power and importance to hidden drives. Intellect detached from these primitive roots was nonsense. As Arp describes it, "Today's reason is a disease" (ibid., p. 341), another echo of Bion's perspective on thinking as a relationship between primitive and higher mental functions through access to the infinite mystical experience of O. Without the complementarity of the mind's dual mental functions, thinking is detached from passion and the possibility of creative thought. This gives rise to Bion's (1970) "thoughts without a thinker", which are not created through reason, but through contact with fundamental truths which exist in that timeless realm. Grotstein (2011) makes the point that these thoughts are not strictly without a thinker, with which I heartily agree. However, it is not the thinker we usually associate with thinking; it is not the ego, but the id, the unconscious dreamer, who receives these unbidden truths.

Arp invokes the same mysterious source for the creative process as Bion does for thinking.

> [Art has] to come forward on tiptoe, unpretentious and as light as the spoor of an animal in snow. Art has to melt into nature. It should even be confused with nature. But this [is] the opposite of naturalistic copying on canvas or stone . . . All one has to do is lower one's eyelids, and inner rhythm will pass purer through the hand . . . the harmonics, the pulsation, the repetitions, and the metaphor of the melody become the rhythm of a deep breath. (Jean, 1974, p. 341)

As the primitive mind "melts" into nature, it becomes capable of access to knowledge beyond that of the ego. One must go to this trouble to get past the "terrifying, threatening . . . machine world" of false reason, which we also so commonly see in patients dominated by the mechanistic anti-knowledge of primitive super-ego (Bion, 1970). Arp's suggestion to "lower one's eyelids" and melt into this natural dream-like state resonates with the capacity for reverie (Bion, 1962a), which facilitates the processing of emotional experience into thought.

Arp said that the dadaist "invent[ed] ways of giving the bourgeois insomnia" (p. xviii), very similar to Freud's (1914d) statement that he, and psychoanalysis, "had come to disturb the sleep of the world"

(p. 21). Both statements make reference to the defensive or pathological sleep that is really a denial, or repression, of the life of the mind.
Paradoxically, once this "sleep of death" (Shakespeare, 1621) is disturbed, once one awakens to the buried feelings, and to the violence
of having buried oneself alive with them, one must find a way *back*
to sleep, to the capacity for reverie and the healthy repression of an
adequate barrier between conscious and unconscious life. As Bion
(1978) says, "You can't forget anything which you can't remember"
(p. 41). Therefore, one has to remember it, bring it to consciousness, in
order to forget it. To go to sleep is that kind of healthy forgetting
which is the source of alpha function, dreaming, and the waking sleep
of dream-like reverie.

Arp's idiosyncratic uses of language represent waking dreams that
emanate from an unconscious beyond time and space. Dada laid the
foundation for the abstract movement in art, and Arp's writings blur
the boundary between reality and phantasy, between sense and
nonsense. The word "dada" itself is meaningless, and in the following
piece Arp seems to "conjugate" this nonsense word. Treating words
as non-lexical sounds and rhythms, much the way babies hear
language, he closes the gap between the adult mind and the primitive
mind of the infant.

> The statue lamps come from the bottom of the sea and shout long live
> DADA to greet the passing ocean liners and the presidents dada a
> dada the dada the dadas I dada you dada he dadas and three rabbits
> in india ink by arp dadaist in porcelain of striped bicycle we will leave
> for London in the royal aquarium ask in any pharmacy for the dada-
> ists of rasputin the tzar and the pope who are valid only for two thirty.
> (Jean, 1974, p. 3)

There might or might not be sense intended in these non-linear
images, which might or might not lend themselves to accurate interpretation. Implicit in them, however, is the idea of the importance
of communication beyond reason, the need to stimulate feeling of
unknowing, even confusion, to awaken the sleeping thoughts. These
prose poems, spoken by "arp dadaist" rather than Arp of the "real"
physical world, were "transcribed directly, unreflected, and uncor-
rected" (Jean, 1974, p. xix). This kind of surreal automatic writing has
the intention of communicating directly from the unconscious to
escape the domination of the shrunken ego. We can try to interpret it

like a dream or like the blots of a Rorschach, but, lacking more information, the following ideas are merely impressions and conjectures
based on my own associations.

The lamps that at the "bottom of the sea shout long live DADA"
evoked for me the idea of illumination gained from contact with that
primal oceanic infinite. The presidents, popes, tzars (and parents)—all
the powerful grown-ups who dominate society—are themselves often
unknowingly dominated *by* this dark unknown area of primitive dada
dreams and half-sense. Unconscious of that infant self, however, these
leaders and pillars of society could also be dominated by the primitive superego, which seeks to dominate and oppress those turbulent
primitive parts of the personality. The "cures" of power and false
reason over this unruly realm are temporary, for ignorance of the
watery mental depths of the "aquarium" renders the power of Ras-
putin and his ilk irrelevant except for a historical instant ("two
thirty"), while the artist's dada dreams provide the experience of eternal truth.

Arp's writings evoke the sense of mystery of that eternal realm,
along with the confusion, uncertainty, and disorganisation of this
experience beyond the so-called "rational" mind. There is almost a
violent rejection of sense, implicit in which is the looming presence of
the violent oppression against emotional freedom of that diseased
reason. Arp's works seem to suggest that by building up a tolerance
for the simultaneous sense and nonsense of the mind, one might learn
how to dream while awake, which is the real foundation of reason and
thought.

> I like to reckon slowly slowly
> but incorrectly . . .
> Likewise I like to
> reckon painstakingly
> without obtaining any result.
> (Jean, 1974, p. xviii)

In analysis, we also reckon very slowly within the waking dream
of mental states of not knowing and becoming. There, our desires to
be "correct" ensure that we will be wrong, as the reaching for answers
obstructs knowledge gained through an experience of being, of O.
Only in that process, without imposing one's will toward any particular result, can those subtle unknown ideas emerge to find a form.

CHAPTER FIVE

"O": the spiritual aspect of being

"There are not enough mystics and those that there are must not be wasted"

(Bion, 1970, p. 80)

"One must be a diver in order to discover the pearls; and not every diver will find them, only a fortunate, skillful one"

(Rumi, 1994, p. 195)

Bion (1975) defined mystery as:

> ... the capacity to have feelings of respect for the unknown... not to be so frightened of what we do not understand [in people] that we want to say, "'Oh, I don't know what he's talking about—put him in a mental hospital' or ... 'let's have him executed'. (pp. 55–56)

The infant who lacks adequate emotional containment does just this to himself, locks up or murders the unknown mystery of his feelings, while silencing those aspects of his mind open to knowledge of unknown mysteries.

As we have seen, the prohibition against knowledge is a theme in the myths of Genesis, but the distinction needs to be clearly made between this primitive anthropomorphic God opposed to truth and the concept of God as a representation of metaphysical truths. The judgemental wrathful God who suppresses curiosity and truth is the punishing internal God of Bion's (1962a) primitive "super-ego" whose stance is "an envious assertion of moral superiority without any morals" (p. 97). This internal God opposed to emotion is anti-knowledge and cannot think, and for the patient dominated by this God, any attempts by the analyst to shed light on the personality are fiercely resisted. On the other hand, Bion makes it clear that access to religious feeling is central to human experience, as well as to the concept of O.

> Psychoanalysts have been peculiarly blind to this topic of religion. Anyone, recalling what they know about the history of the human race, can recognize that activities which can be called religious are at least as obtrusive as activities which can be called sexual . . . One wonders on what grounds a mind or personality could be regarded as a human personality or character if it had missing one of the main departments of mental activity. (Bion, 1974, p. 15)

The distinction between the mystical experience and the dogma of organised religion was expressed succinctly by Nietzsche (1882), "The religious person is an exception in every religion" (p. 185). While he often expressed his hatred of Christianity, it was from the perspective that only those of deep faith could afford to question the hardened beliefs that obstructed the deeper knowledge of true religious experience. Lou Andreas-Salomé, Nietzsche's friend and later Freud's patient and *protégée*, saw in Nietzsche "a heroic trait" which she connected to that religious sense. He was still an unknown writer when she predicted he would become "the prophet of a new religion" (Peters, 1962, p. 123). But Nietzsche was seeking a new kind of faith based on knowledge, whose purpose was to affirm and celebrate all of life's power without denying the senses and sensual pleasure, a sense of religion as an integration of higher knowledge and primal experience. Bion expressed similar ideas, and *à propos* of these statements, Grotstein (2007) said that his personal experience of Bion led him to wonder whether Bion was "not only an analyst but a Zen master" (p. 33). These opinions are not meant to deify Bion or

Nietzsche, but to note what seems in each to have been a dedication to exploring the mind's metaphysical mysteries.

Although Bion's concept of O opened psychoanalytic thought to the exploration of spiritual knowledge, the aim of this discussion is not to bring religion to psychoanalysis. Rather, it is to clarify that psychoanalysis, as a science of the mind, is a science of spiritual proportions, and that this perspective is an essential part of analytic work. Bion pointed out that the tendency to view religious feeling and faith as supernatural might simply reflect "a lack of experience of the 'natural' to which it relates" (Bion, 1970, p. 48). One had to include an awareness of the natural human experiences of curiosity, awe, wonder, love, devotion, which are beyond sensual reality. Nietzsche (1885b) also makes this clear, writing, "The 'kingdom of heaven' is a condition of the heart – not something that comes 'upon the earth' or 'after death'" (p. 147).

Freud's (1927c) perspective on religion as an illusion and a neurosis has guided analytic thinking away from religion as a central human issue, contributing to this vast area of mental experience going largely unexamined. In exploring the differences between traditional religion and the mystical traditions found in Eastern and Western gnosticism as further illustrations of O, religious traditions will be examined through the lens of science and reason, and the rational scientific discipline of psychoanalysis will be examined through the lens of religion.

Mystical traditions

Rumi notes the difficulty in expressing verbally the metaphysical reality of "God".

> The word comes from Soul,
> But is embarrassed in front of Soul . . .
> To know and talk about wisdom
> Is an honorable torch.
> But in front of the Sun of Truth,
> They become embarrassed and disappear.
> The world is like foam.
> The sea is like God's attributes . . .

> Don't bother with the foam.
> It is all embarrassed by the sea.
>   (Rumi, 1993a, p. 27)

Rumi's comparison of the physical world to "foam" on the surface of the transcendent sea is a strong image, a world that is as ephemeral as the most ephemeral metaphysical experiences. However, while our paltry words used to describe this divine essence are an "embarrassment" next to the thing itself, verbal language is recognised as the best we have, an "honorable torch" necessary if one is to *approach* the possibility of bringing these mysteries to light. Language, part of the groundwork of the capacity to think, makes these experiences thinkable, and so the development of language is critical to the capacity for conscious contact with this numinous state.

Rumi's use of the word "God" reflects the tenets of Sufism, Islamic gnosticism dealing with mystical states. For the Sufi, God is not a material being, but a metaphor for Divine Qualities (Helminski, 1993), and Sufism was considered a science aimed at an experience of subtle knowledge. Its aim was to help one "die to the self . . . abandon the ego and be born again to the spirit" (Thackston, 1994, p. xxiii). Rumi's poetry is described by Helminski (1993) as "an elaboration of an instant hereness, the immediate inner song of experience that floods this world but is not of it . . ." (pp. 8–9). This is an accurate description of O, which also reflects Rumi's concept of God as a metaphysical state.

In Eastern philosophy, the gateway to higher perception requires suspension of the mask of the ego, the false persona. To the Hindus, this leads to contact with one's true self, the *Atman*, or universal spirit of man. The *Atman* is equivalent to the supreme spirit of God, or Brahman, a non-dualistic view in which man is one with God as an infinite principle rather than a supreme being. This differs from the beliefs of the Catholic Church concerning the Eucharist, where the transubstantiation of bread and wine is felt literally to convert those substances into the body and blood of Christ. Given the Hindu view of the self as equivalent to the divine spirit, it is not surprising that the writers of *The Upanishads*, the Hindu text, were not religious men, but thinkers and poets familiar with the shifts from everyday consciousness to poetic or spiritual vision (Mascaró, 1965). Analysis requires this same mental shift as the analyst enters into that non-dualistic state of being—O—in order to make contact with the patient's essential being.

Brahman is seen by most Hindus as an ineffable God who cannot be named, much like *Yahweh*, the Hebrew God whose name it was blasphemous to utter. The exact etymology of the word "Yahweh" is unknown, but it is believed to have originated from the Semitic root "hawah", meaning to be or to become (Mettinger & Cryer, 2005). Given this sense of a process of being or becoming, the orthodox Judaic interdiction against uttering God's name seems to be a corruption of the metaphysical idea that the name *cannot* be uttered because it is a numinous experience beyond the purview of language. As Rumi's poem described (above pp. 59–60), any word used to represent such a vast concept simply dissipates like foam. Like the reification of the concept of God, belief in the interdiction against the word—Yahweh or G-d—shifts awareness away from the existence of an unknown and unknowable reality. The idea of an ephemeral state of being devolves into the concrete notion that it is a sin literally to *speak* the name.

With that reified God, an *idea* of an unknown infinite principle is distorted into a persecuting personal God into whom is projected that frustration of not knowing and the hatred of the intolerable mystery. This externalised hatred of frustration is now feared as an angry God opposed to divine enigmatic knowledge. The individual's dread of the return of the unknowable formless infinite O is feared as an outside force. These feelings, which cannot be "suffered" (Bion, 1970) mentally, are experienced as imposed by an external superego God responsible for one's suffering.

This reified idea of religion was, rightly, viewed by Freud (1927c) as an illusion. However, his view of God as a representation of the child's primitive perspective of an all-powerful father did not include a metaphorical idea of God as a representation of fundamental knowledge (cf. Reiner, 2009b). Grotstein clearly expressed Bion's belief that "Freud never understood the power of man's religious instinct" (Grotstein, 2007, p. 31). Bion (1992) acknowledged that if, as Freud said, religion was an illusion, it was, nonetheless, "a basic illusion . . . a very powerful force" (p. 374) which existed from birth, and such an essential part of human experience was unnatural for analysts to ignore. He addresses the primacy of this transcendent spiritual experience with the idea that "The idea of infinitude is prior to any idea of the finite" (Bion, 1967, p. 165).

À propos of these dual perspectives of the concept of God, Bion (1970) states, "What is to be sought is an activity that is both the restoration of God (the Mother) and the evolution of god (the formless, infinite, ineffable, non-existent), which can be found only in a state in which there is no memory, desire, understanding" (p. 129). One cannot skip the personal primitive relationship to the mother and expect to achieve an evolution to the state of being and mindfulness which, paradoxically, is based on the capacity for what might seem to be the mindlessness of that state beyond memory, desire, and understanding. Plato (380 BC) reflects on this contradiction, suggesting that God took away the minds of poets so that they might better express His. "The deity has bereft them of their senses" (p. 220). He describes the poet as "a light and winged thing, and holy, [he is] beside himself, and reason is no longer in him" (ibid.). The poet is not identified with reason, with the ego, he is "beside" or outside of that self, he becomes one with "God's" mind, a holy mind "bereft of its senses", a state of mind beyond memory, desire, and understanding.

A famously anonymous fourteenth-century Christian mystic called this natural/supernatural state of mind the "cloud of unknowing" (Walsh, 1981). To achieve this primal state of unknowing, a state like the "emptiness" Matisse described as part of creative expression (above p. 11), one was directed to seek God not through knowledge, but through blind faith, a "cloud of forgetting", analogous to the suspension of memory, desire, and understanding. Bion describes receptivity to O as an article of faith, but makes it clear that, in his view, this experience of faith is "a scientific state of mind" (1970, p. 32). It is faith in the existence of these essential truths which present themselves to the mind which is open to think them.

Gnosticism

Conflicts between the ideas of God as a metaphysical experience and the reification of God as a physical entity have existed in religions of all kinds throughout time. The traditions of gnosticism are reflected in the metaphysical perspective of O. The word "gnostic" is based on the Greek "gnosis", meaning knowledge, or cognition, and the Christian Gnostics, like the Sufis, were a mystical sect whose religious perspective was based on knowledge rather than superstition. Considered

heretical by the early church, their focus was on the spiritual knowledge embodied in Christ's *ideas* rather than in the *body* of Christ.
While there is some disagreement as to the exact dates the Gnostic
gospels were written, the earliest estimates of these ancient scrolls
place them no later than AD 120–150, some time after the Christian
gospels (estimated to have been written between 50–100 AD). Some of
the traditions found in them, however, pre-date the New Testament
(Pagels, 1989, pp. xv–xvi). Discovered in an Egyptian cave in 1945,
these gnostic texts—the Gospels of Thomas, Philip, Mary, and
others—differed fundamentally from the gospels in the New Testament. The Gnostics viewed Christ not as a deity, but as a *representation* of essential spiritual wisdom, and his teachings were viewed as
the ideas about this numinous realm (Pagels, 1989). Christ himself was
not the saviour; his *ideas*, rather, were the means by which one might
rescue his or her true self from ignorance or unconsciousness. In the
Acts of John, a well-known Gnostic gospel, Jesus equates himself with
knowledge, entreating his followers to understand, "To you as Logos
I [was] sent by the Father" (ibid., p. 89). The Father, too, was a reflection of divine knowledge.

Like the analysand's idealisation of the analyst, which serves as
resistance to the painful work of learning, the process of learning
about the self and inner world is devalued in favour of fusion with a
divine being.

It is hard to know how much of what is written in the New Testament is due to the distortions and corruptions of the early church.
There is controversy, for instance, about whether Christ's resurrection
was meant as a literal fact or a symbol, and there are discrepancies
about this, sometimes even within the same gospel. Some statements
clearly indicate that this was viewed as a literal event. After the
Resurrection, for instance, Christ tells Luke to touch him, saying, ". . .
a spirit does not have flesh and bones, as you see that I have" (Luke
24: 36–43). In Mark, however, it is said that Jesus "showed himself
under another form" (Mark 16: 12). Christ's appearances in the Gnostic texts, on the other hand, are viewed consistently as visions or ecsta-
tic trances, i.e., as *mental* acts. In the Gnostic gospel of Mary, Mary
Magdalene asks Jesus directly if one sees such a vision through the
soul or the spirit, to which he replies that the visionary perceives
through the mind. In another Gnostic gospel, Christ explains, "I am
the intellectual spirit, filled with radiant light" (Pagels, 1989, p. 13).

Although the ideas might seem the same, the material view predominates in the New Testament. The Biblical version, "I am the light of the world ..." (John 8: 12), suggests an equivalence with the light, while the Gnostic version of Jesus as "filled with light" describes someone who is a vessel for "light", or consciousness.

While each person can bring either a concrete Fundamentalist or symbolic metaphorical understanding to what is found in the New Testament, the Christian orthodoxy clearly refuted the "heretical" views of the Gnostics, whom they called atheists (Pagels, 1989, p. 83). The Gnostics, on the other hand, considered the Christians to be "prisoners ... without perception" (ibid., p. 112), imprisoned in the limitations of the body and physical existence, for they failed to see Christ as primarily a representation of the spirit.

There are many other signs in the Bible, however, which point to the symbolic meaning of God as a metaphysical state. When Moses asks God's name, for instance, God (Yahweh) replies, "I Am that I Am ... you must tell the sons of Israel: I Am has sent me to you" (Exodus 3: 14–15). This suggests the metaphysical consciousness of an unnameable state of being, or becoming, beyond the concrete physical entity.

The distinction between a religious *feeling* of awe in the face of unknown mysteries, and the transmutation of that feeling into the belief in an anthropomorphic God reflects the difference between symbolisation, and the concretisation of a symbol that Segal (1981) called a symbolic equation. In the latter case, a symbol is experienced as equivalent to the thing it represents. Bion sheds light on these mental functions with reference to normal symbolisation and psychotic symbolisation.

> The symbol, as it is usually understood, represents a conjunction which is recognized by a group to be constant; as encountered in psychosis it represents a conjunction between a patient and his deity which the patient feels to be constant. (Bion, 1970, p. 65)

Again, the reification of God substitutes for a capacity for a mental experience, an absence of the capacity to think. The psychotic symbol is a primitive attempt to manage or give meaning to an emotional experience by attributing it to the opprobrium or approval of a personal God. It reflects the primitive view of God rather than the mystic's symbolic view of transcendent knowledge, a distinction

Symington (1994) eloquently makes between "primitive religion", driven by a primitive belief in an external deity, and "mature religion", an inner experience of religious feeling.

Clinical example

This next clinical example illustrates the fear of an internal primitive God that militates against the pursuit of truth and knowledge and a sense of being.

"Greta"

"Greta" was regularly beaten as a child and escaped from her feelings of terror and helplessness into a state of isolation and superiority. After ten years of analysis, she had developed her own successful business. She began to understand her confusion between good and bad, in her awareness of a punishing internal voice that judged her every thought and action. It was a constant struggle in every session as to whether she should listen to what I said, or listen to this voice warning her not to listen to me. It was a fierce battle between the life and death of her self. By the time of this session, however, she had challenged the power of that voice enough to have become painfully aware of feelings of need for me, and for other people.

She spoke today (a Monday session), of feeling lonely over the weekend, and angry with herself for having isolated herself all her life. She described intense sexual feelings for an employee at work, which felt inappropriate and alarming to her. She dreamt,

> I saw Henry Lieber, an old friend, he was very glad to see me. Then I noticed a huge storm brewing. I was staying in a hotel but they changed my room. I was put in another room, which seemed to belong to someone else, and their "stuff' was all over the place. I was upset, I was sure I wouldn't be able to sleep there.

She liked Henry, she said, but rarely saw him, as he lived out of town. She commented on her sensitivity to other people's feelings and did not like clutter around. I thought that the "selected fact" (Bion, 1962a, p. 72), the key to the dream and to Greta's anxiety, was that she had "changed rooms". Her intense loneliness had to do with a sense of separateness, of having moved out of her womb-like isolation into a place where there was evidence of other people. Being in the real world among real people was felt to be a bad thing, according to that God-like voice warning her against contact and truth, although it offered the possibility of a new *mental* space which allowed for relationship and passion. In support of this idea, I thought there was a pun in her friend's name, "Henry Lieber", *lieber* meaning "love" in German, which made reference to the connection and love she had intermittently begun to feel for me, and for her friends. She rarely saw "Lieber", for she rarely saw love, since the violence she had experienced as a child had caused her to retreat from such intimate connections. Reactivating even these pleasurable feelings of attachment and love had created in her an emotional storm, which, to her primitive baby self, felt like undifferentiated mental *clutter* she could not even recognise as her own feelings. These unknown unmanageable mental states had been sexualised and displaced on to her employee at work.

Until now, Greta's "God" had been that God-like superego self which warned her against feeling, contact, and knowledge. Truth was hated, and the lies that protected her from the pain of reality were embraced. Having dared to challenge this voice of isolation and ignorance, she is, nonetheless, terrified that changing to "a new [mental] room" will disturb her sleep. Of course, she is right. In fact, her "sleeping" feelings have already begun to awaken, and to awaken *her* to the chaotic storm of primitive feelings she has in relation to real people.

The infant as mystic

Bion's (1970) discussion of "The mystic and the group" outlines the effects on the group of knowledge gained at the higher level of the mind. The kind of vision characterised by contact with O is described as that of a "genius", "messiah", "mystic", or "exceptional individual" (ibid., p. 64). This person threatens the stability of groups which, as Freud (1930a) described, are dominated by primitive impulses ". . . led almost exclusively by the unconscious . . . [with] no critical faculty" (pp. 77–78). There is no autonomous mind, that is, and no capacity for separateness or being. Like Greta's dreaded change to "a new room", which puts her in touch with her separateness, the new vision of the mystic or genius might reveal the members of the group to be

separate individuals whose needs and feelings conflict with the established order.

Bion (1992) addresses the conflicting aims of groups and individuals with reference to Darwin. "Darwin's theory of the survival of the
fittest needs to be replaced by a theory of survival of the fittest in a
group" (p. 29). With incisive irony, Bion describes the basis of the individual's survival in the group as

> . . . an ability to see what everyone sees . . . to believe in survival of the
> dead after death in a sort of Heaven or Valhalla or what-not . . . an
> ability to hallucinate or manipulate facts so as to produce materials for
> a delusion that there exists an inexhaustible fund of love in the group
> for himself. (Bion, 1992, pp. 29–30)

The individual who lacks these "abilities" to dissemble, hallucinate,
and turn away from his own truth might be forced to destroy his
awareness of the group's indifference to his individuality and his selfhood, and to destroy his fear of the group to which this indifference
gives rise. Those able to tolerate the truth, however, as Greta has
begun to do, find the strength of mind to stand up to the conservative
tendency of the group and embrace their own separate identity, without which there can be no change or growth.

The analyst sees patients every day who unconsciously forfeit their
autonomy as individuals, renouncing their minds and selves in order
to preserve the illusion of a harmonious and cohesive family group.
The infant's oneness with primitive mental processes makes him an
"exceptional individual" in the conservative environment of the
group, and might pose a challenge and a threat to parents who have
split off the primal experiences which are precursors to their own
exceptionalness. This kind of family group, installed in the infant's
mind, becomes an internal voice against authenticity and selfhood,
obstructing the capacity to contain the deeper truths that form the
foundation of mental wholeness.

Cassandra is a mythological prototype of the mystic's (or infant's)
plight. The Greek daughter of Priam, king of Troy, Cassandra was
endowed with the gift of prophecy, but fated by Apollo never to
have her prophecies believed. She was, thereby, forced to endure the
frustration of knowing truths ignored by the larger group. For the
infant whose deeper emotional experiences go unnoticed, the connection to these truths erodes and the potential for a real self languishes,

becoming the source of emotional dissonance in the child and/or in the family.

The group can destroy the new awareness through hatred or through idealised love or deification of an individual or an idea. The analysand who idealises the analyst as a God, also idealising himself in the process, destroys the treatment as certainly as the analysand who attacks it directly. To bear the new idea is to endure the sometimes dizzying oscillations of an experience of change and mental birth. Like the "storm" in Greta's dream, emotional change feels chaotic, catastrophic to the known self, but the containment of these conflicting dualities of inner and outer reality are the essence of wholeness and being.

> The man of God is drunken while sober. . ..
> The man of God is perplexed and bewildered. . .
> The man of God is a king clothed in rags. . .
> The man of God is neither of earth nor fire. . .
> The man of God doesn't read with his sight.
> The man of God sees good and bad alike.
> The man of God is far beyond non-being . . .
>
> (Rumi, 1993b, p. 60)

CHAPTER SIX

The language of being and mental wholeness

Georg Groddeck (1929), the self-proclaimed "wild analyst" (p. 7) much admired by Freud, wrote: "Life obliges us all to make use of words, and to believe that because we use them we are therefore always aware of the meaning bound up in them" (ibid., p. 33). Groddeck examines how our use of language relates to the deepest meaning of the self, referring specifically to the distortions created by one's lack of understanding of his or her inner life. He looks at the word "I", for instance, a word he deems necessary to exist in society but which, at a more fundamental level, presents a false idea of the individual's separateness from the outside world. Dividing the world into "I" and "Not-I", he suggests, expresses an unfounded belief in the power of one's will, when, in fact, one's life is directed by an unconscious force. He called this force the "It" (in German, *das Es*), a word Freud (1933a) borrowed from Groddeck for his theory of the "id" (p. 72). While his theory sounds like Freud's idea of the unconscious, Groddeck clearly distinguished the two, stating simply, "Psychoanalysis is not the same as studying the It" (1929, p. 43). According to Groddeck, the ego (*das Ich*, or "I myself"), is created by the It, so that one cannot properly say, "I live", but, rather, must say, "I am lived by the 'It'" (p. 41). This is a more passive, less wilful ego, and Freud quotes

Groddeck's idea when he says, "what we call the ego behaves essentially passively in life" (Freud, 1923b, p. 23). Again, this loss of power over the self has a great deal in common with Freud's idea of the unconscious. Both render the individual a more passive player in his own life and mind, but, for Groddeck, the power of the It has a more essential meaning which imparts a different role to the ego. In his view, the ego is "a mask used by the It to hide itself from the curiosity of mankind" (Groddeck, 1929, p. 41). From this perspective, one's primary identification is with the It, from which evolves one's primary sense of self. In a sense, the ego is an *acquired* or created self, as opposed to an experience of something fundamental and universal that extends beyond, and perhaps originates from beyond, the boundaries of the self.

In Groddeck's view, the truest and most essential 'I' is the metaphysical 'It', not the ego, whose job it is to hide or control that vastly greater mental/spiritual unconscious. Despite their theoretical differences Freud's admiration of Groddeck was reciprocated by Groddeck, who saw psychoanalysis as a revolution that provided "the best way of approaching the It" (p. 41).

In many ways, Groddeck's ideas are closer to those in Bion's concept of O, which I would say does include the force of Groddeck's "It". Groddeck characterises the It as the "coherence of the universe ... which endured from everlasting to everlasting" (pp. 36– 38). Like Bion's concepts of O and proto-mental thoughts", as well as Plato's notion of pure forms and Jung's idea about archetypes, the It was seen to exist before birth, even before conception.

As Groddeck suggested in his discussion of the word "I", much of our confusion when it comes to language and communication reflects the misperceptions of inner life, in particular the acquired self, which functions as a mask for the truth. Our efforts to think are hampered, that is, by our lack of emotional understanding of who we are at the deepest levels of existence, and so *problems of language are inextricably bound to problems of identity, and problems of thinking itself.*

Many of the clinical examples we will look at in the ensuing chapters reveal the ways in which unexperienced and unthought primitive experiences obstruct development of the true self. In Groddeck's terms, one is cut off from the "It" and left with the persona of a "shrunken ego" by which one navigates within society. The job of the ego is to hide—especially from oneself—the fact that one's mind, thoughts, and words do not express one's essential meaning. In listening to some patients, we might sense that their words seem meaningless, as if falling from their mouths like ashes, the remnants of a powerful internal sun no longer able to fuel the mind. In the actual celestial sun, the fusion of hydrogen atoms into helium is the source of its enormous energy. If one is mentally split from the It, one's powerful source of emotional enlightenment, the energy of the personality is generated by a kind of mental *fission* rather than *fusion*. This mental energy derived from splitting and detachment from an authentic emotional self leads to disintegration and the frenzied movement of excitement or mania. It leads to darkness and mindlessness, rather than mental integration and illumination.

We might compare this idea of fusion to Bion's (1962a, 1963, 1970) ideas of a link based on love (L) or knowledge (K), while fission represents attacks on linking. The mind cut off from its primary source of energy—the unharnessed power of the It—replaces experience with the destruction of experience, "K" with "−K" (Bion, 1962a). Bion's analytic elements of L, H, and K represent emotional connections derived from the relationship of container and contained, the binding together of feelings and thoughts. Bion (1992) uses the example of the destructive God in the Babel myth as "an attack on linking—[on] the language that makes co-operation possible" (p. 241).

Bion's ideas about dreams and his theory of container and contained help us think about how this primal force can be harnessed into thinking. Freud (1900a) views dreams as expressions of phantasy and wish fulfilment, whose aim is to reduce tension by repressing unwanted truths. This differs significantly from Bion's (1992) perspective of dreams as a means of unconscious thinking, a means of bringing to conscious waking experience hidden truths which cannot be mentally accessed or processed without the function of dreaming. This distinction is made clear by Freud (1933a, Lecture XXIX) who says, "Processes which take place in the system unconscious . . . are quite other than what we know of our conscious thinking" (p. 17), further stating that the unconscious instinctual impulse, which is the creator of the dream, "cannot strive for anything but its own satisfaction" (p. 18). According to Freud (1933a, Lecture XXXI, p. 73), "the logical laws of thought do not apply in the id", but Bion's view of the unconscious suggests that while the truths presented there might not be logical in the same way as the (shrunken) ego, they have a kind of logic which represents higher forms of truth.

Bion pointed out that waking life, and thinking, are more depen-dent on dreams than had been appreciated. He referred to the "dream-work" as the processing of waking experience (through alpha-function); the dream, in essence, is doing the work of trying to reveal itself to the ego. Freud (1933a, Lecture XXIX), on the other hand, defines the "dream-work" as the process of the ego's disguising or repressing material by making it unconscious. The analyst's work was then to undo the dream-work in order to make "the now incom-prehensible dream comprehensible" (Bion, 1992, p. 43). The difference in their views is clearly expressed in Bion's statement, "Freud says Aristotle states that a dream is the way the mind works in sleep: I say it is the way it works when awake" (ibid., p. 43). Rather than func-tioning as a means of *hiding* truth from oneself, dreams help to reveal truth and to process it, and it is the ego, rather than the id (or "It"), which drives the attempts to hide it.

The mask of the ego

This poem by Tagore, the twentieth-century Bengali mystic, expresses the fallacy of the ego's power.

> He whom I enclose with my name is weeping in this dungeon. I am ever busy building this wall all around; and as this wall goes up into the sky day by day I lose sight of my true being in its dark shadow. (Tagore, 1913, p. 45)

The poem goes on to say that he takes pride in the wall. However, the other face of this apparently protective wall, or mask, is the cruel superego, which forbids contact with the emotional self in order to deaden the painful feelings and hide one's true self in an insular state of mind.

Behind the wall is the creative self (the It, or dreaming self) strug-gling—in this case through poetry—to escape this self-imposed prison. Antonin Artaud, the early twentieth-century French *avant garde* playwright, wrote, "No one has ever written or painted, sculp-ted, modeled, built, invented except to get out of hell" (Des Pres, 1988, p. 138). Artaud's "Theatre of Cruelty", as he called it, aimed at forc-ing the audience out of the complacency of the imprisoning masks they themselves do not know they are wearing in order to restore a sense of passion. The incarceration in this deadly prison is an attempt to limit or control the infinite, unknown It.

Like Groddeck's notion that the word "I" falsely separates one from the world, Tagore describes his prison as his *name*, which limits one to a single persona. We can compare this with the freedom of the metaphysical self expressed in Rumi's poem (above p. 68), where the confinement of this imposed limit gives way to the oscillating dance of simultaneous emotional states. The idea of that confining self *vs.* a state of freedom and being is also beautifully expressed by Emily Dickinson.

> I'm nobody! Who are you?
> Are you nobody, too?
> Then there's a pair of us—don't tell!
> They'd banish us, you know.
>
> How dreary to be somebody!
> How public, like a frog,
> To tell your name the livelong day
> To an admiring bog!
> (Dickinson, 1959, p. 75)

By giving up that known and limiting ego, one dares to be the "nobody" capable of contact with the essential unmanifest self. The latter is a state of becoming, the constant process of change and continuous transformations of a mind unlimited by the boundaries of a calcified persona. To "tell your name to an admiring bog" is to accept the fixed social values of that frozen self, "saturated" (Bion, 1970) or "bogged down" with expectations, memories, and desires. Bion (1970) describes the shortcomings of this saturated state. "An analyst with such a mind is one who is incapable of learning because he is satisfied" (p. 29). It is a primitive state of a memory full of projections and evacuations, of which Bion says, "Such a 'memory' is no equipment for an analyst whose aim is O" (p. 29). O, in Dickinson's terms, is the capacity to be in that state of open-ended becoming, that is, to be "nobody".

Art and psychoanalysis as mental containers

An unsaturated mind that provides an open space for authentic experience and new truths also presents a daunting emotional challenge.

These previously unknown truths require a means of containment, and artistic expression, like dreaming, allows one to give form to otherwise unmanageable feelings. As Nietzsche (1888) put it, "We possess art lest we perish of truth" (p. 435, aphorism 822).

Both art and psychoanalysis are interested in truth, and both give form to otherwise formless experience; both are engaged in changes which emanate from that vast essential "It"—Bion's (1965) "transformations in O"—rather than from the confinement of a rigidly "intellectual" ego. We can say that both art and psychoanalysis provide the possibility of an escape from the mental prison of the mask, but, clearly, there are differences in their methods and perspectives, as well as their effects upon the mind.

While both provide an emotional experience which can help release the artist and his or her audience into an emotional and metaphysical state of mind, because analysis takes place in the transference, it does so in a way that is effectively different. As a re-enactment of old feelings for the parents in the present interaction with the analyst, the transference relationship has an affective immediacy and specificity that engenders contact with a different aspect of the mind. For one thing, this kind of emotional *relationship* is an encounter with a living human being, and the analysand is not just a generic audience member, both he or she and the analyst are participants in the drama. The analyst's capacity for the wakeful dreaming of reverie helps him to inhabit the mental space—the O—of the analysand. The analyst is in a position to reflect upon his own experience of the patient and communicate to him specific and *personal* experiences evoked in the process. This uniqueness and specificity makes it possible to illuminate emotional information about the particular primitive parameters of the prison in which the individual has incarcerated himself. In being personal, it is both more alive and more threatening. It also has the potential for more effectively stimulating change, as the specific primitive emotional experience can be contained in a specific thought. This goes beyond an emotional experience, as a mental container for thinking can be created in this integrative process. This is not true for everyone, and certainly there are those for whom the experience of a film or piece of art creates more movement than an analysis.

Once again the issues of language and communication arise. Despite the usefulness of the poet's tools of metaphor, analogy, and myths to communicate something of the patient's essential numinous experience, these very methods of clarifications can induce new obstacles. Bion describes the paradoxical limitations of trying to clarify something through the use of a metaphorical story.

> I may be able to make [something] clearer while at the same time being misleading. Alternatively, I can resort to something which is so sophisticated that it has very little or no feeling . . . I can either be comprehensible and misleading or truthful and incomprehensible. (Bion, 1974, p. 24)

The trick, it seems, is to engage both functions of container and contained, emotion and reason, in a working relationship with each other.

Clinical example

The question raised in the following three sessions with "Leslie" is, to whom is one actually speaking to, the patient's mask or a real self in a state of being/becoming? The sessions are not consecutive, they took place over a period of three weeks, but they show a shift over time from a closed down self incapable of real transformation to a more expansive and present self. Again, these shifts inevitably shift back, although with each one something is learnt of one's relationship to these aspects of the self that might (or might not) have a cumulative effect.

"Leslie" is a middle-aged, currently single, singing teacher who has been in analysis four to five times a week for ten years. She grew up with an emotionally overwhelmed mother and four sisters whom she felt she had to protect from their physically abusive father. He had beaten the mother, and once beat Leslie badly enough to require a physician's care. In addition to all this, there was some early sexual abuse by a close family friend.

Leslie: Session 1

"Leslie" complained of exhaustion relating to her work. Although she enjoyed it, she felt the emotional challenge that came with absorbing her students' frustration and resistance, although she also recognised it as a necessary part of the creative process. She had two dreams.

> I had been asked to assign a group of people to different beds. I didn't know why I was doing it but I was good at it and that felt good.
>
> I then dreamt of my friend, Andrew [a ballet dancer she greatly admires]. His every move was graceful, and conscious.

She said that Andrew was always aware of his body in time and space. His ability to catch and lift his partner required his full presence and attention, and she knew she could not be present in this way. This was something that had been coming up in her treatment lately, and she said today how bad she felt about how she keeps resisting my help. "But I can't help it," she said. Andrew had recently told Leslie that he admired her insight into her students' feelings, which made her feel good. She knows she is good at her work, she said, but then found herself unable to tell if Andrew's comment was really true or not. She did not understand why she was assigning people to beds in her dream, but had a thought about all her sisters in their respective beds as children.

Leslie's uncertainty about her work revealed her confusion about her worth, but also about her own thoughts, which she cannot trust. She does not really know what she thinks or feels. Leslie took care of her sisters as a child, as she now does with her students, and I thought that her mysterious talent for assigning others to beds had to do with having identified with a care-taking mother, to rid herself of her neediness and confusion. From this perspective, the four beds seemed to represent the four "couches" of her four analytic sessions, and that she was assigning her students to her sessions with me. She was "assigning" them her helplessness, need, and resistance as well as my interpretations, thereby disseminating and diffusing any help she got from me, keeping none for herself. She had projected so many feelings and fragmented her mind to such a degree that, unlike her dancer friend, she could not be present in her body, or in her mind. She could not, in other words, be. As a result, despite her intuition into others' feelings, she never really knew what she felt or what was real. With a mind that could not function as a healthy container for truth, she existed in a no-man's-land of doubt.

I thought that Andrew also stood for me, and her admiration included feelings of envy of me as someone she felt was capable of being present. Leslie was envious that in this "dance" we are doing together, I could be present enough to "catch" her, to hold her mentally, which she could not accomplish for herself. As difficult as the dancer's feat is, the mind presents a vastly more complex challenge, for, if one slips, there is no physical pain and no visible evidence of damage. Leslie's pride about her "talent" at doling out beds was the pride of having created this method of bypassing her painful feelings of need, admiration, and envy toward me by doling out these feelings to her students (sisters, and others). She was then the teacher/mother/analyst, but unaware of the unconscious damage to herself, and to the me in her mind. Her admiration of me was based largely on her sense that I could tolerate being in reality, while she, with only a mask to substitute for a real self, had no way really to be or to think for herself.

Leslie: Session 2

Leslie felt frightened as she had begun to have feelings which felt beyond her control. In this session, briefly described, she was disturbed by a dream in which

> she'd been ordered to make a bomb. She later learnt it would be used to kill children and innocent people, and she felt horrified that her lack of awareness would result in such a terrible thing. Even if she were never found out, she thought, "the people would still die".

It is worth noting that Leslie sounded completely different to me in this session. She was upset, but sober and grounded. What I was hearing seemed to me to be the sound of truth, a moment of contact with O. Unlike the feelings of disconnection in Session 1, there was a sense of real suffering, which made my emotional reaction to her different as well. I felt more empathy for her today, instead of the sense of coldness engendered by her detachment. The horror she felt in the dream about her unconscious actions were evidence of what felt like an incipient conscience, that whether or not she consciously knows what she is feeling and doing, it is, nonetheless, real in her mind. It felt like a kind of awakening, acceptance of the fact of her own mind as a reality, an awareness that truth exists whether or not she knows it. In essence, it is an awareness of her own existence, which includes awareness of the consequences of phantasy and inner intentions as well as actions. I thought that these ideas were played out in the next session.

Leslie: Session 3

This third session with Leslie shows a further development that I thought reflected a deep proto-mental level of her mind. Over the past month or so, as Leslie's mind continued opening up to her emotional experience, she had intermittently begun to have what she called "a cellular feeling", or "a cellular reaction", to my interpretations. Her whole body felt responsive, she said, and she "felt" a deep understanding that she could not necessarily think or talk about. It did not feel to me like resistance, but like an ability, finally, to stop listening to me from the perspective of the controlled mask of the ego, allied with her judging superego. Our interactions had ceased to feel emotionally detached or intellectual. This might sound like a small shift, but it felt vast to me and often catastrophic to her.

Leslie had been talking for several days about adding a fifth session, as the weekend gap felt too long between appointments. She reported this dream.

> I was having sex but I was seeing the intercourse as if from inside my vagina, I could see the penis and vagina coming together. I felt very open to it, open to sex, not judgemental at all.

In the previous session, she had dreamt about

> a house by the beach which she was thinking of buying. "It was a mixed picture," she said, "there were beautiful things, like a really nice pool and a living room with a great couch in front of a fireplace, but there were other rooms with lots of clutter and mess . . . like my mother's house."

Mentioning the lack of judgement in today's dream was a reference to the jealousy that has often come up about her parents' sexual relationship. Leslie mentioned that she did not know who she was having sex with in the dream, but that "It was a dream thing, like maybe I *was* the intercourse . . . I can't really think about it . . . I'm having that cellular feeling." Her tone and the image did not have the feeling of the baby's jealous phantasies of intruding on the parental couple. She spoke of her desire to meet a man and have sex, but I understood her "cellular feeling" to reflect a proto-mental experience of allowing the penis and vagina to come together, as she had been allowing us to come together for analytic intercourse. Whether it was actually a proto-mental "memory" of her own conception I certainly could not say with any conviction, but I expressed my thought that she seemed to be acknowledging that her parents had a sexual relationship, which had resulted in her being conceived and born. In the transference, I felt reasonably convinced that it reflected the changes I felt in the last session, as well as in this one, the result of her allowing herself to be emotionally engaged in our analytic intercourse. She replied, "I was thinking yesterday that I loved my father." I was surprised to hear her express any love for a father whose abusive rage she had always felt so poisoned by, and after a pause she added, "Just saying it now makes me sick."

On rare occasions, Leslie's dreams had allowed her to recall some feelings of admiration and love of a little girl for her father, but she could entertain them only for a moment before her hatred surged up and she became nauseated. In this context, I surmised that Leslie's feeling of love might have reflected a more primal experience of "love", an innate preconception of an emotional and mental link connected to life. I considered that it might be the natural and essential instinct for life at that deeper proto-mental or cellular level *before* the experience of an abusive father, and before the enormous rage which had led her to deny her parents' and her own existence. The earlier untarnished capacity for "love" represents the innate, even instinctual, capacities for mental and emotional attachment. The later reaction, secondary to this instinct, reflects the complicated confusion about love and hate, life and death, of the abused child. Further "evidence" for this view was based on my experience of this patient over the years, which left me with no doubt about her powerful connection to life, despite the daunting forces against it.

These are subtle distinctions between the implicit primal memories of the womb *vs.* the unconscious *phantasies* of a protective womb later developed as a defensive retreat due to early trauma. I thought this distinction was reflected in Leslie's dream of the previous day—the "mixed picture" she had described of her mother's house by the beach, cluttered and messy, but with its lovely couch by the fire. On the one hand, we might consider this as a representation of a proto-mental foetal "memory", which carries the pre-traumatic possibilities of her instinctual mind, her inherent potential for wholeness. This conflicted with her post-natal memories of disturbed mother whose mental clutter and abusive behaviour had led to Leslie's retreat to an encapsulated womb to escape the abuse. These differing mental states are characterised, on the one hand, by love and connection, on the other hand, by hatred, which leads to the flight from connection. It seemed to me that in this session Leslie was experiencing those more primal "cellular feelings" as a yearning for her connection to me, the nice analytic couch by the warm fire where she was beginning to entertain her own existence.

The confusion of that natural state with the defensive retreat into a phantasied womb, however, is never far behind. It is hard enough for me to talk of it here and, understandably, Leslie could not yet distinguish these extremely subtle internal experiences. Nonetheless, I think it is an important distinction to make, for it addresses the question of how to begin to disentangle the patient's proto-mental experience of a womb as the source of life from which one can go forward from the pathology which keeps the patient stuck there. However, regarding Leslie's dream about "being" the intercourse and her association to loving her father, there seemed to be clearer evidence that through the painful awakening of her feelings, at least for this moment in the analysis, Leslie had been conceived in our combined mind.

The Language of Achievement

The sound of truth I heard in these last two sessions exemplifies Bion's (1970) ideas about the Language of Achievement. He bases this term on Keats' (1817) idea of a "Man of Achievement" (pp. 328–329). People like Shakespeare, Keats said, exhibited what he called, "Negative Capability", the ability to exist in "uncertainties, mysteries, doubts, without any irritable reaching after fact and reason" (ibid.). Negative Capability is equivalent to that state of being in essential reality (O), like Dickinson's "nobody", who is actually the metaphysical self. The presence or absence of this state can be detected in language, in the non-lexical aspects of speech. The Language of Achievement is distinguished from the Language of Substitution—"language that is a substitute for, and not a prelude to, action" (Bion, 1970, p. 125), and Bion points out that the inability to discern which of these one has encountered in the session can lead to analysis interminable (ibid.). Session 1 with Leslie (above, pp. 75–77) was characterised by the Language of Substitution, lies and evasions that I experienced as a state of torpor and stasis and irritation. This shifted in the subsequent sessions to a capacity to speak from a real self.

The perspective of creative work might help in distinguishing between words spoken in a state of authentic existence and those detached from the self and so from reality. Words, as they are used in poetry, are often functions of the Language of Achievement. They might sound different than words used in everyday speech, as if the words themselves have undergone a transformation and deliquesce into a new form appropriate for use in a poem. Of course, the words themselves do not actually change; it is their *usage* which is different, a function of the writer's mind. This idiosyncratic usage leads to changes in the meaning of what these words express.

Pound (1934) describes great literature as "language charged with meaning" (p. 36). The power of this charge comes through three basic ways, which he calls phanopoeia (visual image), melopoeia (the sound, or music and rhythm of words), and logopoeia (groupings of words) (p. 37). The latter refers to the poet's use of words in different configurations, often daring usages of words in unexpected contexts and unexpected relationships to other words. This capacity comes about in the contact with the numinous realm, and gives rise to a unique voice that can express a unique individual mind. These words, derived from the Language of Achievement, serve as a kind of action that can emotionally and mentally move or awaken the willing listener to an experience of that realm.

The following is a poem I wrote, again long before I had consciously examined these ideas about language.

How To Speak

> Speak,
> where words stalk like animals
> and you are the prey.
> To those who need mothers, speak,
> to criminals, to babies
> and to yourself, speak
> like the trees, speak
> knowing it doesn't matter what you say,
> it is the music, the juice,

the love and hate that try to mate
but stay on either side of their own lines
and you in the middle
speaking.
Speak of where you are,
where you are is where you're going;
speak your parents on their own road
driven by passion;
speak loud
and clear
though words come apart like water,
the sun shining through them.
And then . . .
stop speaking.

(Reiner, 1990, p. 13)

The elusiveness and insubstantiality of words that originate in that dream-like cloud of unknowing, while ephemeral, might, paradoxically, have more presence and impact than the common usages of words. These words, which "stalk like animals", are emanations of the untamed It that directs one's life and mind. Speaking as the poet, one feels the power of those words and the experiences from which they emanate as if one is being preyed upon by an autonomous power over which one has no control. In hearing it, however, one may find a way to tame it sufficiently to express something of those veiled realities. These kinds of words have the energy and movement of a mind suffused with emotion, as the poet's creative mind (O) reveals things to the poet that he does not consciously think. As the poem above suggests, the words themselves feel somehow fluid, as if they have no fixed meaning and no substance, and so are capable of coming apart and being reconfigured to produce new meaning based on their source in an unbounded matrix of associations.

One can only wonder at how these "action words", which feel as if they have an energy of their own, find other words which connect and produce meaning, sometimes even for other people, and it is this mystery which makes the poem effective or meaningful, despite its non-linear means. It is the same mysterious method by which the analyst's mind, in a state beyond memory, desire, and understanding, encounters the connections between the patient's non-linear associations that enable him to hear the selected fact. In that supra-rational state, as in dreaming, one's experience shifts from the causal connections of waking life to the experience of timelessness and relative meaning in a space–time continuum. The latter is a mind which is nowhere because it is everywhere, a part of the infinite reality of evanescent change and impermanence.

The poet's experience of a surge of unbounded energy rises up to create associations, metaphors, or symbols whose relationships transcend the rational meaning of the words. The words of the Language of Achievement might be compared to a forty-ton whale suddenly in flight as it breaches the water, giving those words a sense of great weight and meaning which is simultaneous with a sense of weightlessness.

While language often seems to come naturally to human beings once they have learned the basic vocabulary and rules of grammar, the Language of Achievement, with the power to express metaphysical truths, requires the kind of emotional birth and sense of being or becoming we saw in the clinical examples. In addition, it needs constantly to be reinvented, and this is a capacity that frequently eludes us. People know the literal meanings of words, but the uses to which they are put can drain the words of meaning. The Language of Substitution, reflecting a mental state characterised by mindlessness and distortions, obscures emotional states and destroys the connections engendered by those emotions. Words used in this way lack the ephemeral lightness addressed in the poem above, they feel weighted and meaningless and, like Bion's (1963) beta elements, they are of use not for abstract thinking, but only as evacuations of unthinkable states of mind.

O: the poet's Muse

The gifted poet can recognise in his work the power of the Language of Achievement to move the reader, or patient, into the realm of connection, passion, and life. Ideally, the same is true of the analyst, who, one hopes, can also come to recognise when his or her words are "lies" which substitute for this capacity. For the great artist, the life force, with this capacity for mental freedom from conventional or dead language, is often balanced by an equally morbid experience of mental or emotional death. The work of art can help one to gain dominance over those forces of death and restore him to a state of being. The artist is no more susceptible than others to such dark feelings, but might retain the capacity to be open to them, in which resides the potential to overcome them. As Trilling (1950) described it, "What marks the artist is his power to shape the material of pain we all have" (p. 175).

Neither poets nor psychoanalysts can sustain that challenging state of contact with a state of wholeness and being where the Language of Achievement prevails. Like the artist who must court the Muse, the analyst must continuously evoke this state of reverie beyond memory, desire, and understanding in which transformation can take place. Even Shakespeare, who probably used language in a more sophisticated way than any writer who ever lived, also provided relief from the work of sustaining this elevated language of the higher mind capable of containing such profound ideas. His often coarse or primitive comic relief, ostensibly for the plebeians in the audience, was probably for himself as well, for even the greatest artists are earthly physical beings who cannot exist constantly in the spirit, or, as Rilke describes it, among the angels.

Rilke: the poet of life and death of the self

In the *Duino Elegies*, Rilke (1912b) frequently uses the symbol of angels. In the famous first line of the "First Elegy" he writes, "If I cried out who would hear me up there among the angelic orders?" (p. 19). In the "Second Elegy", he writes, "Every angel is terrible. And still, alas knowing all that, I serenade you, you almost deadly birds of the soul" (p. 27). Rilke described these "angels" not as those of Christianity, but as "that creature in whom the transformation of the visible into the invisible which we are accomplishing already appears in completion . . . [it is a] recognition in the invisible of a higher order of reality" (1912a, p. xv). This invisible realm of the "It", or O, is commonly viewed as an encounter with one's own destiny, with being, or with the Muse. These "angels" are terrifying indeed, at least to our logical earthly selves, for, while they function as liaisons to the divine made manifest, they also present us with feelings of mysteries beyond our knowledge and control. Rhode (1995) writes, "In terms of Bion's theory of truth, a mediaeval theologian might have described thoughts as angels who are reluctant to be embodied. These angels are the mysterious thoughts as yet unthought, in search of a thinker (Bion, 1997, p. 27).

Rilke's legendary inspiration, which gave birth to the *Duino Elegies* and *Sonnets To Orpheus*, might be described as his version of Christ's Passion, for almost directly after completing these works Rilke became ill and was dead within three years. His exhaustion, chronic stomach problems, and loss of weight were later presumed to have been leukaemia, among the symptoms of which were also painful, bleeding black pustules on the mucous membranes of the nose and mouth (Leppman, 1984, pp. 375–384). It seemed like poetic injustice, imposing a painful and punishing silence after his brilliant verbal communication.

It sounds almost like a punishment from an Old Testament God for whom mortal access to the divine knowledge of those angelic orders was forbidden. But we might also look at the "great giving", as Rilke called it, as a last heroic burst of life mobilised against an unconscious premonition of the deadly illness already growing inside of him. There is no way to know, but we do know that this poet of life and death endured a mighty and ongoing internal struggle between these two mental forces all his life. After that great inspiration, this most famous of hermits called himself,"infinitely immoveable, a prisoner of myself in my ancient tower" (ibid., p. 373), a sort of pendulum swing back to the forces of silence and death. We see these pendulum swings all the time in our patients who venture into an authentic experience of the self. The next chapter is an exploration of how this integration of dark and light forces of consciousness and unconsciousness begins to develop in the capacity to contain primitive mental processes in thought.

CHAPTER SEVEN

Being and non-being: a clinical view

B ion was realistic and straightforward about the limitations of the practice of analysis. Asked whether he was optimistic about getting patients to submit to the analyst's inevitable invasion of their minds in the service of relieving them of pain, Bion (1978) said, "No, I am not optimistic about it, although I think it is on the right lines" (p. 9). Such humility about our work as analysts is always refreshing, for accepting a patient into one's care is a great responsibility and there is a natural desire to *want* to help, and to *believe* one is helping, rather than harming the patient, or being ineffectual. These are among the desires that Bion suggested suspending in the session if one were to be available to whatever truths might emerge in the course of treatment, for no matter how much the analyst or analysand may want a guarantee of success, whatever that might mean, neither of them can know the eventual outcome of the treatment.

This reality is the source of great anxiety for every patient. Although often unconscious, it reveals itself in endless ways which need to be addressed. One patient, whom I had been seeing for a few months, remarked one day that he trusted no one. I pointed out that being "someone" myself, this obviously included me. He agreed, then asked directly whether I could help him, to which I replied that I did not know, it depended on him and it depended on me, and on the work we did together. For the first time he seemed to relax. He had fully expected reassurance, which he rightly would not have believed, and he was relieved to hear the unpleasant truth rather than a pleasant lie. This said something for the patient's regard for truth, despite his view of analysis as a bunch of malarky, and for that moment he did trust me. Unfortunately, he had little regard for that part of him which valued truth or trust, and after three years he quit. The patient's true feelings were terrifying to him, and I accepted that he had made the right choice for him. That did not mean that I saw it as he did, simply that it was not for me to say. The truth could be so feared that the patient might rightly sense that he cannot tolerate it. On the other hand, a patient's false self might be so profoundly cherished that the individual chooses to remain loyal to it. The outcome of treatment, therefore, also depends on the patient's capacity and/or desire for change, and on other factors about which neither analyst nor analysand has any idea at the outset. Although we as analysts have our biases, the fact is, one does not even know what will constitute "help" for any particular patient, and, as things progress, patients might change their minds about whether stepping into their own lives and their own selves makes the challenges and the pain worthwhile.

I say this as a prelude to this chapter, devoted specifically to clinical work demonstrating the lengthy, labyrinthine process of coming into being. It includes detailed work with dreams in order to help recognise the absence of a sense of authentic being, and how it can develop in the oscillating movements between being and non-being. Although previous chapters have already included clinical examples, some of these are consecutive sessions, which help get a specific sense of that development, and the terror which accompanies this psychological birth of new and unknown states of mind. Because of this more intensive examination, I thought it would be useful to say a few words generally about clinical technique and to elaborate my own clinical perspective in particular.

Notes on clinical technique

My approach to a session is influenced by Bion's (1962a) idea of the "selected fact" (p. 72), an organising element around which the session coheres. He borrowed the term from Poincaré, who described elements of a mathematical formulation which were ". . . scattered and seemingly foreign to each other [but which] suddenly introduce order where the appearance of disorder reigned" (Bion, 1962, p. 72). Bion (1992) called the selected fact the "harmonising or unifying fact" (p. 44) in the session, capable of bringing order and sense to an often overwhelming amount of material. This organising fact might easily get lost in the mass of associations. Mysteriously embedded in the session, it presents itself to the analyst's mind just as mysteriously from amid the unconscious ephemera of the patient's communications. Its "arrival" into the analyst's awareness depends upon his or her ability to endure the chaotic disorganisation of O as he listens to the material, bolstered by the faith that such an organising function exists. Faith in the existence of truth facilitates the analyst's patience to endure that chaotic uncertainty without "any irritable reaching after fact and reason" (Keats, 1817, pp. 328–329). The selected fact escapes unbidden from the patient's mind like an image from a dream, and can only be grasped through the analyst's similarly dream-like states of reverie and hallucinosis. Bion makes clear the inestimable challenge of this task.

> Being on the right wavelength, which has to be experienced to be recognized, is unfortunately comparatively rare. Nevertheless most patients are able to put up with the rarity of it on the off-chance that we may sometimes succeed. (Bion, 1978, p. 41)

Implicit in this statement is Bion's awareness of the *patient's* recognition that truth exists. In addition to the intuitive capacity for contact with these primitive dream states, the analyst also needs to provide himself with rational evidence as to how this intuition manifests itself in the session. One can, thereby, satisfy one's own curiosity as well as one's own scientific demands for evidence. There needs to be, that is, some sort of technique.

T. S. Eliot described a similar need for some kind of poetic technique, which he saw as the only thing the poet had to reassure himself that he had not simply wasted his life on something as amorphous as poetry. Analysis takes place in a similarly amorphous realm, and, while there are analytic techniques determined by theoretical principles, a large portion of technique is determined by the analyst's personality. Eliot's poems, for instance, do not sound like anyone else's poems because they do not hew to any established technique, but out of the mind and personality of the artist a unique and new technique emerges, in conjunction with that which is being expressed in the moment. From this perspective, technique is a function of container and contained. A new thought creates a new container, and through this relationship, the mind is constantly reinvented and reborn in a new form. The variability in analytic styles grows out of the unique personality of the analyst, determined by that particular relationship between his or her mind (container) and its contents (contained), which includes an infinitely vast amount of unknowable emotional factors.

It raises the question, though, that in the absence of familiar and strict rules and classical forms—sonnet, haiku, Freudian/Kleinian/Bionian analysis, etc.—how does one know that one's technique is valid? For the analyst, the basis of the capacity to apprehend the selected fact lies in the capacity to apprehend the truth, to see things as they are, an obviously challenging endeavour, and one ultimately impossible in any absolute sense. However, the effort is facilitated by having gleaned sufficient evidence to support one's intuition about the unifying element in the session. The integration of intuitive and rational/scientific perspectives leads to a hypothesis which can be examined in light of the evidence. Much of this evidence is derived from emotional reactions of transference and countertransference. Bion (1953) wrote, "Evidence for interpretations has to be sought in the countertransference and in the actions and free associations of the patient" (p. 24). The relationship between the infinite space of the mind and the attempts to represent it in verbal thought with reference to sensual phenomena allows for a transformation into thought. Like thinking in general, it is both frustrating and liberating, but from it truth and meaning can be derived. Bion (1959) described this "conjunction of sense-data . . . [as] . . . a commonsense view" (p. 119), two perspectives which present different but compatible views of the same phenomena—in this case the experience of the patient in the session. The analyst provides himself a second perspective, a kind of second opinion that validates or invalidates the first. At times, Bion used the term "commonsense" in relation to an agreement between different physical senses, but he also used it to refer to this integration of intuition and reason, or other dual functions of the mind.

The following is a description of the physicist's work, which could just as well express the analyst's experience.

> Physicists spend a large part of their lives in a state of confusion . . . To excel in physics is to embrace doubt while walking the winding road to clarity. The tantalizing discomfort of perplexity is what inspires otherwise ordinary men and women to extraordinary feats of ingenuity and creativity; nothing quite focuses the mind like dissonant details awaiting harmonious resolution. But en route to explanation . . . theorists must tread with considered step through the jungle of bewilderment, guided mostly by hunches, inklings, clues and calculations . . . Nature does not give up her secrets lightly. (Greene, 2004, p. 470)

That "jungle of bewilderment" is the confusion of the paranoid–schizoid position into which the analyst is plunged as he or she listens to the "tantalizing perplexity" of the discursive tangle of clinical material. If the analyst can bear the confusion, the selected fact might present itself to bring order. The analyst is rewarded for his efforts by the security of new truths that bring order in his own mind. Bion characterised this transition from disorder to order as an adult equivalent of the infant's transformation from the paranoid–schizoid position to the depressive position (Ps↔D), and described it as a necessary foundation for a correct interpretation. The analyst needed to go through these two phases: first, a sense of persecution (although a form of persecution modified by experience), and then, as he put it, ". . . he must pass through the depression before he is ready to give an interpretation" (1992, p. 291).

Precision of interpretation

There are differing opinions about the importance of precision in making an analytic interpretation. Many analysts believe there is no one correct interpretation. Bion addressed the idea in relation to how the psychotic patient responds to inexact interpretations. "He is very precise, very exact and does not like interpretations which are off the beam; he usually ignores them as if they haven't been said at all" (1978, p. 4). This reaction implies the existence of an accurate interpretation which is recognisable by the patient, in this case a patient who is very ill, but I have found this to be true of many patients, especially those with some awareness and sensitivity to primitive experiences.

Bion (1992) described the analyst's failure to interpret the dream as the most powerful contribution to the patient's acting out, but he expressed other ideas on the subject of dreams in his unpublished clinical seminars in Sao Paulo in 1987. He claimed not to have troubled himself about making "inadequate" interpretations, since he had "never given any other kind" (Borgogno & Merciai, 2000, p. 75), and characterised correct and adequate interpretations as an analytic myth. Psychoanalysis is not, and probably will never be, a "hard science", for the instrument of perception is the analyst's mind, and a more subjective and enigmatic instrument can hardly be imagined. In addition, in dealing with the vast unknowable realm of the mind, the limitations of our understanding do not allow the possibility of a complete interpretation, and yet I do think that the analyst can learn to sense whether his or her interpretation has hit the mark, whether it is received by the patient, and what happens to it after that. It is imperative, in fact, to try to track that which is being enacted emotionally in the transference and in the countertransference in response to one's interventions. If the patient's capacity to think is undeveloped, an interpretation capable of illuminating O could only address that obstacle to truth, and to thinking.

In providing the clinical material, I will try to point out the selected fact which emerges to gather all of the material into a coherent picture or narrative. I have emphasised what I found to be some "hot" words or phrases in an effort to identify the selected fact, those communications which seemed to stand out and draw my attention to them, for such elements often lead the way to more essential emotional depths. As this mysterious word or idea or association slips out from the unconscious and organises the plethora of possible interpretations, one might find evidence for what is taking place at that moment for that particular analyst and patient. I present these five sessions with "Sara" as illustrations of the oscillations between the connection to being and non-being of the self, states of mental life and death.

"Sara": Session 1

Sara is a research chemist in her mid thirties who grew up with a psychotic mother. In analysis for nine years, she presented with alcohol problems and feelings of crippling insecurity. While she no longer drinks, she is often tortured by self-doubt. This first session is described briefly to give a sense of her loyal attachment to an idealised internal mother which erodes the development of a self.

> Sara dreamt of being *inside her childhood home. Outside,* she saw a demonic witch and screamed to her sister, who was also *outside the house,* "Get in the house NOW!" Sara tried desperately to lock the door, but it would not lock properly. "There were *no good locks on the doors* in real life, either," she said.

Sara said it was terrifying. Her thoughts went to a friend who was diagnosed with an *auto-immune disease* for which she had refused to get help. Each part of this dream and the associations in the session seem to cohere around the patient's confusion between inside and outside. Given this central focus on images of inside and outside the house, and the fact that the dream takes place at Sara's "childhood home", the "house" in question seemed to me to represent her mother's body, and a foetal state of mind. It reflects the primitive experience of a baby for whom *inside* and *outside* the mother, and *inside* and *outside* the self, are not yet differentiated.

The infant, naturally, has no boundaries, but with a psychotic mother who also lacks boundaries, Sara had "no locks" to keep out her mother's projections and disordered thinking. Therefore, she lacked the conditions necessary to develop a self or mind, to differentiate self from other, or good from bad. At that level of her personality, she cannot tell if this "demonic" mother is outside her or inside her. Her phantasy that she is inside the mother like a foetus, where she thinks she is safe, is, in fact, her undreamt nightmare of that demonic mother inside her mind which deprives her of any feeling of safety.

If this is the essential idea of the dream, the rest of the elements in the session should be organised around this idea. And, in fact, I think we do see this supported in her associations, for from the perspective of that confusion between inside and outside, self and object, it is Sara who has a *mental* auto-immune disease, she is allergic to her self, to that psychotic mother/self from whom she is undifferentiated. Like her friend who did not want help with her disease, Sara does not want my help. She chooses, rather, to maintain her outmoded belief of being inside a phantasied good womb, although we can see here that

this is the "bad" psychotic internal mother with whom she is identified. However, I thought we could see an unconscious struggle in this
dream, a nascent capacity to think about and distinguish between
inside and outside, good and bad.

Fairbairn's ideas about internalisation of bad objects is helpful in
understanding Sara's difficulty in relinquishing this old attachment.

> In my opinion, it is always 'bad objects' that are internalised in the first
> instance, since it is difficult to find any adequate motive for the inter-
> nalisation of objects which are satisfying and 'good' . . . it is only inso-
> far as his mother's breast fails to satisfy his physical and emotional
> needs and thus becomes a bad object that it becomes necessary for the
> infant to internalise it. (Fairbairn, 1944, p. 93)

Good objects, he adds, are internalised only later on, as a defence
against the already internalised bad objects. This kind of "good"
object would seem to be an idealised object, which only serves to
confuse the issue further. The point here is that these internalisations
interfere with the natural development and functioning of the mind,
which is based on the relationship between the content and structure
of the mind. Fairbairn (1952) described this mental energy as ". . .
inseparable from structure" (p. 149). It is analogous to Bion's idea of
container and contained, the relationship between which facilitates an
experience of O.

This kind of identification with the bad object is the source of the
false self, a façade behind which the true self is barricaded. It is an
identification, really, with a state of non-being. Sara's potential for a
self capable of "becoming" was early on subsumed by the murkiness
of this relationship to a "bad" mother, whom Sara rendered good in
her mind, thereby rendering herself bad.

Sara: Session 2

This session took place one month later, three sessions after a holiday
break.

> Sara dreamt she was dancing with the actor, Kevin *Spacey*, who was
> attracted to her. At first, she was "just kidding around and having fun",
> but when she saw that he really liked her and wanted something more
> serious, she found herself more interested.

As always, the question here is what unites these symbols and metaphors into a comprehensive whole. I was struck by what I thought was a pun in which Kevin Spacey represented the "spacy" mental states in which Sara isolates herself, taking refuge in oblivion and unconsciousness when identified with her phantasy of womb/ mother. The spaciness is that phantasy of foetal oneness we saw in the first session, which destroys the pain of any needs, and any links to an external object, as we see here in her first feelings about Spacey. Her change when she understands he is more serious seemed to reflect an understanding of this deeper part of her—her unconscious—as not only spacy, but also the source of these truths revealed in her dreams.

In her further associations to Kevin Spacey's roles as "sensitive but damaged" men, there were reflections of her own extremely intuitive and sensitive baby self whose capacity for mental growth had drowned in identification with her mindless, spacy mother. With no access to emotional containment or to reason, she had retreated into that primal oceanic mental womb.

This spaciness seemed to me to be the selected fact, the key to the session. As mentioned above, it introduced the idea of a changing *relationship* to that spacy mindlessness, an interesting but complex idea regarding Sara's relationship to her own unconscious. We need to distinguish the spaciness of the unconscious, either as the infant's normal oceanic feeling or the spaciness of oblivion, a pathological defence against feeling. The former represents mental life, the latter, the mental death of attacks on linking.

Sara's relationship to that spacy self was becoming more serious, she was developing interest in having a *conscious* relationship with her own *unconscious*, her own healthy infant self. This was something with meaning rather than the defensive immersion in unconsciousness. What we saw here was not an unconscious dominated by phantasies and delusions of infantile oneness with her mother, but the emergence of a mental integration brought about by awareness of these primitive experiences. This shift is an example of Bion's (1970) idea about the adult version of the transition from Ps↔D, a co-operative relationship between these two aspects of mental life. The binocular vision in which both views work together allowed these conflicting aspects of the self to "dance" together. It also reflects an unconscious that is the source of the wholeness and creative potential of the mind (O), an experience of being.

Until now, Sara's highly developed rational/scientific self has been split from her feeling infant self. In the terror of having a confused psychotic mother, there was no safe place to feel that vulnerable, "spacy", oceanic emotional self, and so her reasoning self could not develop. Each dreaded contact with the other, creating an unbridgeable chasm between reason and the dream-like unconscious. As Spacey becomes "more serious" and Sara becomes more interested in him, she can dance with that "spacy" aspect of her mind.

I did not interpret all of this to the patient in this way, for some of it is for me to think through the evidence, which emerged to me in this session like a dream. The word "spacy" seemed to cut through the fog of my own dream-like, spacy reverie, and carry a different weight than the other words. One can then see how it fits with the other elements in the session and begin to determine whether or not one's idea of the selected fact is accurate. This explanation is an effort to communicate something of the session to the reader, who was not present at the actual session. In fact, it is impossible to translate the session from the non-verbal pictorial language of direct experience into linear verbal language, so that it is now a *representation* of that experience. This kind of transformation is illustrated in a story about Picasso, apocryphal perhaps, after someone criticised one of his paintings. "That doesn't look like a woman," the observer said, to which Picasso is said to have replied, "It isn't a woman, it's a painting of a woman." Likewise, my description of the session is not a session, it is a verbal representation of a session, a very different thing.

My actual experience of the session was not the rational presentation depicted here. Rather, it was of a vast, seemingly pointless collection of words, sounds, images, feelings, and ideas washing over my mind. Whatever "thoughts" I had at that point were the threads of my own ephemeral half-conscious images and ideas, like bits of an invisible tapestry subliminally connecting her mental pictures to mine. At some point during this semi-trance state, the word "Spacey" shone through my own cloud of unknowing. That metaphor from her dream served both as my entrée into her dream and an awakening from my own dream into a more organised state where thoughts could cohere and begin to fashion a key to unlock the meaning of the dream.

In this discursive, dream-like experience, in what Bion (1970) describes as a suspension of memory, desire, and understanding, "thinking" is non-linear. This kind of unconscious thinking that is found in dreams is also experienced in artistic creation. The following poem about the soul (the transcendent self or mind in contact with O) was both *written* in the *process* of that dream-like state of mind (the container), and its contents are a *representation* of something derived from that state of mind (the contained).

The Soul

It's a huge party
where the music plays silently.
Everybody wears a hat.
Everybody's hats have feathers.
Everybody exchanges feathers
and dreams pass back and forth.
Thoughts ripple
in an ocean of wine
where Mind is the absence of mind.
The living and the dead mingle
as equals
and those who are absent are loved,
making them
present.
When the dance begins
a storm of plumes blows around the room.
Everybody is blind.
Everybody suddenly smiles
as each feather settles back
in its original hat.

(Reiner, 1990, p. 35)

Although I wrote this years before I heard of "intersubjectivity", it expresses some of that theory's central ideas about the intersecting minds of self and other, with its basis in an experience of primitive oneness with an object. The words of a poem might seem ephemeral, as if they are not really words at all, but more like the "feathers" in the poem, passing back and forth between minds, or like the dreams in that oceanic proto-mental spaciness which seems to flow or "ripple in an ocean of wine". It also reflects the experience of dizziness which Paul (1997) observed in patients making the mental journey of a psychological birth, the sense of movement patients feel in the transition from a foetal, encapsulated state, to one linked to the feelings of dependency and need experienced for an object in the outside world. Like Sara's "serious" relationship to the spacy, oceanic infant mind, contact with O also includes an experience of boundaries, like the "feathers" in the poem which "settle back into their original hats". It is the paradox of simultaneously having one's mind and losing it in that relationship with an other—the "bit in between" I and Thou. This does not exist in the shrunken ego of Sara's identification with an internal bad object.

Reflections on Sara's dream

Given Bion's idea of dreaming as unconscious thinking, we are called upon to analyse the presence of higher mental functions that the patient is attempting to think about. Sara's dreaming mind succeeded in finding a language in which to think about the experience of her unconscious itself (the container, or what Fairbairn called the structure of the mind), which was also an idea in her unconscious mind (the contained). Clarifying Sara's relationship to her unconscious gave her a chance to begin to be aware of this language she naturally speaks but does not understand, or even recognise as part of herself. While this "natural", or inherent, language has not evolved enough to be consciously thought by the patient, she was now able to "think" it in a dream, to "speak" this natural inner voice more clearly than her earlier dreams could do. She could then see something of what I had sensed in her early on as a considerable potential for integration at a fundamental level of her mind. Both positive and negative aspects of the unconscious are present in the language of this dream, her terror and confusion about the "spacy", disconnected, oceanic feeling of this egoless state as well as its potential for development into a creative mind capable of connection and integration. What this dream illustrated for her is a positive aspect of the terrifying uncontrollable mind and emotional self, which she generally feels anxiously compelled to control and deaden.

Sara: Session 3

This trend toward acceptance of her mind and her own unconscious language becomes more apparent in this next session, one week later.

Sara lamented feeling detached and unable to connect with anyone. She had looked forward to her session today, for instance, but when she got here, she felt fearful of connecting with me, for it meant reconnecting with herself and her feelings. She dreamt:

> I was at my *graduation* from graduate school but it also seemed like the *church* I went to as a kid. I went up and got my diploma, when I got back to my seat my purse was gone. I saw a *big Black man* and thought maybe he'd taken it. But then he picked up his coat and my purse was underneath it and he asked if it was mine. I thanked him.

The Black man, very much like the spacy unconscious, has two aspects. Despite her suspicion, he turned out to be helpful. He did not seem scary, she added, and she was relieved to find her purse, for it had "everything in it, money, ID, everything." She talked about how much she loved church as a child; it was the one safe place, because she felt that if she could be perfect, God could love her.

As in the last dream, there is a sense of growth, a mental shift, "a graduation". I thought her two views of the "Black man" were a way, once again, of including these dual perspectives on her unconscious. This duality was also immediately evident in her experiences of me at the beginning of the session, first as desired, but then frightening. The vast "Black" unknown within her becomes unbearable because of the effect her early trauma in relation to her mother had on her most primal experiences. The "helpful" unconscious—the potential for truth inherent in the experience of O, or the It—reflects a primal experience before the limits imposed on the self by identification with a bad object. Sara is much less familiar with this unknown self, the lost purse in which is contained the truths she both desires and fears.

In this dream, the two experiences of being and non-being, based on Sara's dual relationships to her unknown mind, also include the two versions of God. The God who will love her if she is perfect is that childhood superego God, which, as Freud pointed out, is an identification with the parent. The two aspects of the Black man need to be differentiated: first of all, that suspicious, perfectionistic superego she cannot trust, and second, as the *idea* of a dark unknown but helpful unconscious which connects her to the truth of her self. It is the Black man, after all, who reconnects her with her lost "purse" which contains "everything", the long hidden identity of that primal self.

However, that suspicious and perfectionistic superego God has, all these years, been stealing her true sense of self. Projecting that super-ego God/mother into me frequently turns me into the me with whom she so feared making contact at the beginning of the session.

Sara's dreams in Sessions 2 and 3 help us look at the difference between the wisdom of a higher self—O—and the constricting all-knowing God/self identified with an ideal mother. That repressive superego God is a distortion of the infinite godhead—O—after it has become alienated from its essential nature, and from an infant self capable of growth. The former is the expanding universe of the mind, the latter a contracting or shrinking ego, and the two become more and more alienated until they are unrecognisable as having been cut from the same cloth.

This superego God is the Prodigal Son, the lost son who leaves the Father (God as O), squanders his Father's riches (of knowledge, wisdom), then starves. When he returns repentant, the Father rejoices and celebrates, for his son "was dead and has come to life" (Luke 15: 32). This is the process of mental or psychological birth of an expansive mind with which Sara is grappling.

Sara: Session 4

Sara said today that she could not tell if she was emotionally present or not. By now somehow familiar with the idea of her own emotional existence or non-existence, she can at times have enough access to her real self to intuit that there is a question. Intermittent mental births of painful buried feelings have enabled her to recognise how it feels to be emotionally alive in the pleasure as well as the pain of real contact. As a result, she also feels more fully the immense obstacles she faces in separating herself from her psychotic internal mother, which keeps her detached.

> Sara dreamt she was with young people smoking methedrine. She felt pressured to join them, sensing something bad would happen if they knew she wasn't part of the group. Also, they looked happier as they smoked, so she took a little puff, blowing it out quickly so it wouldn't enter her system. She then wanted more because it relieved her anxiety, but she thought, "No, I don't want that at all!"

In another dream Sara was at a *wedding* of her childhood friend, Gail. Sara said, "My sister and all my friends were already at the reception. Everyone was invited except me, I felt terrible. It seemed wrong to go, but I stayed at the place."

Sara worried that her dream about drugs was a regression to old habits. She recalled feeling jealous of Gail's ability to bond with people in a way Sara never could, and jealous of "normal family" when they were children. Sara had once shared a house with the friends in the dream, along with her sister, whom she described as "crazy". The sisters had fought bitterly, and Sara's friends usually sided with her sister, who seemed rational and controlled while Sara was always so emotional. However, it has become clear as adults that her sister's "rationality" reflects severe schizoid defences that eventually led to a psychotic breakdown from which she has not recovered.

In the first dream, we can see Sara's ambivalence about the drug: she feels pressured but does not want it. I thought that the key to these dreams was in Sara's association that *her friends take her sister's side*. The problem for her is that her *internal* "friends" keep betraying her by supporting her crazy internal sister/mother self. This keeps her divided and confused, unable to know which internal voice to heed. However, there is now also a "Gail" aspect of Sara in the picture, an old internal friend who is in the process of getting "married" to herself, based on her capacity, at least intermittently, to bond with, or be analytically "married", to me. The problem here is that Sara has not been invited to her own wedding. Still split, she keeps betraying whatever bond she makes, "smoking meth" with these so-called friends, destroying her awareness and her mind. Thus, she marries her "crazy" sister/psychotic mother and divorces her thinking/ feeling self. We can see her struggle to maintain her connections, to be a real friend to herself, and despite not having been invited to the wedding, she does decide to stay. We might say that she was never invited to "marry" or bond with her mother, only to fuse with her in the oblivion, the drugged spaciness of her mother's lack of mental boundaries. At that infantile level, Sara has not yet been invited to life, and in the transference she remains on the outside of her own wedding with a mother/me who will not marry her. But she has not given up, and oscillates between her desire to bond with me as a separate person and her desire for oneness in the pathological, and very familiar, spaciness which denies her mind.

This session provided some insight into one of the obstacles in Sara's treatment, which was that what she learns in the session often seems to dissipate when she leaves. Her view of me is, therefore, extremely unstable, still shifting from idealisation to vilification. If she does not yet know who her internal friends are, the experience of learning, of taking in an interpretation, is immediately usurped by the gang of mindless, meth-smoking friends. In order to stay loyal to them, she cannot make use of the treatment. Today, she sensed this dilemma at the beginning of the session and asked herself whether or not she was actually present. At the end of session, I pointed out that it is not just a question for her of "To be or not to be . . ." but a question of what it means "to be" and what it means "not to be".

Sorting out the forces of mental life and death that are so confused in Sara's mind is very complex, for, while I read the dream at the time as her attempt to distinguish the two, from another vertex, she might experience me as the methedrine which she warns herself against as it puts her in touch with her primitive confusion. She becomes consciously aware of that confusion, her inability to tell whether she is present, or absent in some sort of oblivious fog. At this point, we can only return to the session with intellectual conjectures which lack the immediacy of emotional experience, although thinking about it in hindsight keeps one aware, as Bion said, that there is never an "adequate", or complete, interpretation.

Sara: Session 5 (six months later)

By the time of this next session, briefly recounted, there had been quite a bit of development. Her capacity for O—what we might call "mindful spaciness"—was greater, and the fierce resistance to O was clearer. I have included this session because it helps to see what effect the parent's emotional neglect has on the capacity to experience being—O.

Sara had received an important recognition for her work. "It's great!" she said. Then she stopped. I had the sense of a Black Hole. I thought that the honour felt "great" to Sara's knowledgeable self, but to the old, primitive self it had no meaning, not as if it were bad—it was nothing. I suggested that her good news felt to that old part of her that it had not happened at all, as if it had gone into a Black Hole where nothing could escape. She said, "I felt that with my mother all the time, as if everything that happened went into a Black Hole and then it was as if it never really happened." Clearly, she, too, had ended up in that Black Hole.

> I dreamt I was in my home town about to get on a train. Alice, the nurse from my internist's office was there, and she kept saying we should get on the train. She kept waiting for me but I kept missing the train. The first time it was because I saw Nan [an older woman of whom she is very fond], talking to Jimmy Stewart. I was watching them and thought it was nice they were so in love, but Nan felt guilty because they were both married to other people. Then I saw a dying man at the station, but I thought, I can't help him, I have to make the train . . . I don't know if I got on.

Sara did not know where the train was going, but she was disturbed by her "cold" lack of compassion for the sick, dying man. She said she liked Alice, who was "kind and helpful". My thought was that I was Alice, and, since Sara does not know where she and I are going in the analysis, she keeps "missing the train". I keep waiting for her, but first she gets caught up in watching her idealised internal parents who are so in love with each other, leaving the real (sick and divorced) parents in favour of this phantasy. Her confusion becomes clear, for if the man is her sick mother or father, she feels so guilty about letting that part of her mind die that she again misses the train to do the real work with me. In this fear of reality (O), everything is turned backwards. Like the internal friends who lead her astray, she has compassion for the part of her which wants her back in the Black Hole, trying all the time to pull her away from life. I pointed out that her occupation with death leaves her unable to work with me, or to have her own life or mind. After a silence, she replied, "I love and hate what you're saying right now . . . I love that you can see this and that my mind could come up with a dream like this, but I don't like it!"

Sara's ongoing dilemma is her love and hatred of truth: she loves and hates feeling, life, and she loves and hates death. However, as she said, her mind was able to dream this. She was able to represent this essential conflict mentally, to communicate it to me so that I could communicate it to her to think about. This is quite different from the experience that emerged at the beginning of the session in which Sara's experience of life—her experience of O—was negated by the Black Hole of her mother's unconscious mental absence. With that ongoing trauma, Sara's hatred of her own experience was set into motion, often dominating her natural and intrinsic love of and potential for truth—O.

Being and the desire for non-being

Freud's death instinct describes a desire to return to an inanimate state. Bion describes the fear and hatred of the mind and the desire to give up the daunting task of becoming a conscious, sentient human being. Both represent states of desire for non-being, but Bion makes it clear that this is a mental state fearful of truth, and of the mind which houses it.

> [As an analyst] I have rarely failed to experience hatred of psycho-analysis, and its reciprocal, sexualization of psycho-analysis . . . [T]he human animal has not ceased to be persecuted by his mind and the thoughts usually associated with it . . . Therefore I do not expect any psycho-analysis properly done to escape the odium inseparable from the mind. Refuge is sure to be sought in mindlessness, sexualization, acting out, and degrees of stupor. (Bion, 1970, pp. 125–126)

Being and non-being in Beckett

This state of mindlessness and non-being is expressed in Samuel Beckett's (1957) apocalyptic drama, *Endgame*. Hamm, a nearly blind old man living in an empty room in the middle of a dead environment, reminiscences to his slave/helpmate about the past.

> "I once knew a madman who thought the end of the world had come . . . I used to go and see him, in the asylum. I'd take him by the hand and drag him to the window. Look! There! All that rising corn! And there! Look! The sails of the herring fleet! All that loveliness! [Pause.] He'd snatch away his hand and go back to his corner. Appalled. All he had seen was ashes. [Pause.] He alone had been spared. [Pause.] Forgotten. [Pause.] It appears the case is not . . . so unusual." (p. 113)

Hamm lives in the stasis of mental death, having destroyed the world in phantasy, and the world of his mind. He cannot stand to look at the devastation, which he assumes to be real externally, and goes back into the corner, into that entombed state of a womb-like phantasy, antithetical to life and connection. The child who fears that his unconscious rage has destroyed the whole world—his whole family and himself—finds any evidence of life or love too painful to entertain, lest he risk becoming conscious of those long-buried destructive phantasies. As we saw with Sara, any progress toward emotional awakening brings an equal but opposite yearning for the stasis of a deadened mind.

We might presume the madman in Hamm's speech to be Beckett, who himself experienced a severe mental breakdown in the 1930s. As is well known by now, he left Ireland, and his complicated relationship with his mother, to seek treatment in London with a young Wilfred Bion. After reading a new biography of Beckett in 1978, I mentioned to Bion that I had learned of his experience with Beckett. He replied, in his wry and humble manner, "I don't believe I helped him" (1977c, Los Angeles, private conversation). This appears not to be entirely true, judging from the plays Beckett produced in the 1950s and 1960s after his treatment with Bion, works such as *Waiting For Godot, Endgame,* and *Happy Days,* among others, which reflect profound insights into primitive mental life. Beckett doggedly pursued treatment, and yet he described his time with Bion as a never-ending "squabble" (Bair, 1978, p. 197).

Beckett also described being greatly affected by a lecture Jung gave at the Tavistock in 1935, which he attended with Bion at the end of his analysis. Jung (1968) spoke of a child patient who had died but who "had never been born entirely" (p. 107). Beckett was struck by this idea, and began to understand his fears about leaving his bed as his own fixation to the womb (Bair, 1978, p. 207). In Beckett's play, *Happy Days* (1961), the main character, Winnie, is buried up to her waist in a mound of grass and dirt, a depiction, I thought, of this unborn state. As the second act begins, the mound has risen and she is now buried up to her neck, a bold statement by Beckett about the intransigence of these states of mind, which we also saw so vividly in Sara's struggles in the clinical examples. In this predicament, Beckett's character, Winnie, struggles to overcome the meaninglessness of her life. In her efforts to remain cheerful, Winnie reminds us of the child who puts on a happy face in an effort to hide his despair, rage, and confusion in the face of unbearable reality.

"Gwen": Session 1

These two consecutive sessions with "Gwen" are interesting in show-
ing how, paradoxically, an awareness of non-being can represent an
experience of being. The dreams in both sessions deal with the issue
of emptiness. Like Beckett's Winnie, Gwen has spent her whole life
trying to remain cheerful in order to deal with a deep hidden emptiness, but, as Bion (1992) wrote, "What is falsely employed as a substitute for the real, is transformed thereby into a poison for the mind" (p.
299). Gwen suffered early, unthinkable losses, her mother at birth, and
her father at age two. She is an intuitive, engaging, successful woman,
but in an often well-disguised emotional detachment there is an insid-
ious sense of that mental poison. Interpretations often elicit a chilling
empty silence, in which I often have the sense I have shocked her and
plunged her into that unthinkable void.

Gwen was recently divorced from Seth, whom she discovered had
been lying to her and unfaithful throughout their five-year marriage.
Her trust was shattered, and her disgust and despair alternated with
her insistence that she loved him. She felt lost, but stayed with him,
unable fully to convince herself it was true. I pointed out that she was
now also lying to herself, and that Seth had represented this aspect of
her that does not recognise or value the truth. She felt devastated to
learn that it was she whom she could not trust, that she could not
believe her own thoughts, but it enabled her finally to leave him and
to begin working on herself with new earnestness.

> Gwen dreamt of Seth's old friend, Jimmy Ponder, who told her that Seth
> was so broke he couldn't even buy a sandwich. She then saw Seth sitting
> in an empty apartment with no furniture; he was empty inside as well.

Gwen liked Jimmy, unlike Seth's other friends, and described him
as "thoughtful". She felt sad for Seth in the dream, but once awake,
she did not see why she should care. It made sense, however, if he
represented that unavailable aspect of herself which is starving and
empty. This was her infant self starving for a mother. Having become
alienated from her feelings, she had lost her self along with her
mother. Unable then to take in or "eat" whatever food/truth was now
available, she was still starving.

I thought the selected fact in this dream was a pun on Jimmy's last
name, "Ponder", for it is this "thoughtful" man who relays the

message to her about her empty Seth self. I suggested that it is this "ponderer" in her mind who *can* actually think about that self which feels so alone and empty, having been so long buried, or, in this case, projected into Seth. As Gwen thought about this, her whole body relaxed and sank into the couch. We could both see this as a devalued aspect of her mind, but an important one, since it was her only means of communicating with her starving self. Apparently only this "ponderer" knows or can know where she really is. Despite the painful awareness of how lost she had been emotionally all her life, Gwen felt hopeful at experiencing something in her that can inform her of where she is. One might expect this hopefulness to have another side, which we see in the next day's session.

Gwen: Session 2

Gwen dreamt that she was

> in an empty space. She was upset to learn that she had a $20,000 debt about which she knew nothing.

Gwen was reminded of yesterday's dream, except that now it was *she* who was in the empty space. She then went on to talk about some good developments at work, and I sensed that she had slipped away emotionally. It was difficult for me to focus on what she was saying, it sounded as if she were no longer listening to herself, as if that "pondering", thinking self was gone, and I was put in the role of the unavailable self or partner who was not listening to her either. Both of us were meant to be mindless. I said that I thought she felt the need to evade the feelings that had come up yesterday, as well as those in today's dream. Like the cheerful Winnie in *Happy Days*, she had switched mental channels, away from the feeling of emptiness to a happy chat about work. She replied quietly, "If I'm with someone who's listening I'm accountable." She clearly did not like this feeling, and, after a silence, she added, "I don't want to learn these things."

Immediately, her heart started racing; a moment later she felt frozen. I thought that suddenly finding herself present had stimulated the feeling of her birth, the surge of anxiety at finding herself in that endless empty space without a mother. Petrified, she had immediately frozen these unmanageable feelings of loss and terror, turning away from her emotional self. With no one to hear her, she had stopped listening to her own pain. Essentially, she had lost her mind, or the potential for a mind, her undeveloped capacity to "ponder" that we had seen yesterday, and that apparently still resides somewhere in her.

After these interpretations, she returned to her dream. "This empty space was even emptier than the one in yesterday's dream," she said, ". . . this wasn't just an empty apartment, it was a void." We could then see what she was evading. She had moved from that vast empty space without her mother to an even emptier space of her own creation, a void, de-void even of her own feelings. This amorphous emptiness was meant to be a safe womb, but it had no location and left her with the hopelessness of no real contact and the despair of never being found.

Gwen associated the debt in her dream with Seth's having been out of work so that it was left to her to pay for the construction of a new nursery in anticipation of plans to have a baby. She now felt enraged at him for allowing her to go ahead with this since he was already cheating on her. I interpreted that the debt in the dream which she *did not* know about was what she owed to her own baby self that she had left behind in the void, the same baby self she continued trying to a-void today. I said, "You seem to feel the need to pay off this debt so that perhaps you can be the baby, and the person, you were born to be." She now sounded sober as she replied, "It sounds so simple . . . but it's so hard to do." I could not have agreed more.

Bion (1992) uses the words "vacancy" and "minus" to describe this state of emptiness, which only appears to be an absence or vacancy. In fact, as he points out, it is not really empty. "'Vacancy' consists of greed, envy, hate, destruction, paranoia" (ibid., p. 300), all the primitive reactions which had led to Gwen's terrifying and infinite void. Her capacity to ponder, the essence of her desire for truth, remained an undeveloped aspect of her personality, usurped by unconscious lies. In experiencing the emptiness, her own sense of non-being, she finds that undeveloped aspect of her still alive, and begins to experience something of what it means to be.

CHAPTER EIGHT

Duality and the myth of Sisyphus: a clinical exploration

"It is possible to be mad and unblest, but it is not possible to get the blessing without the madness; it is not possible to get the illuminations without the derangement"

(Norman O. Brown, 1960, p. 2)

"The minute I'm disappointed, I feel encouraged.
When I'm ruined, I'm healed"

(Rumi, 1984, p. 16)

Humpty Dumpty Had a Great Fall

Humpty Dumpty didn't realize
that to fall to pieces is to write a poem,
a poem whose words, like dreams,
don't know what they're saying—
they're just dancin'!—
and those who learn to dance understand them.
After the Fall, Humpty Dumpty became a great poet,
but none of the King's horses and none of the King's men

ever understood his work.
He died, a broken egg,
unappreciated in his lifetime
but later discovered in a rare and used bookstore
when his book of poems fell off the shelf
and hit me in the head.
I was concussed
and rushed to the hospital.
When I awoke the book was there,
beside my bed,
so I read it
and was so moved
I fell to pieces.

(Reiner, 2002)

The "fall" in this whimsical poem is the source of a creative act, and so the seemingly traumatic dis-integration might not be so bad after all. It is a matter of perspective, for that "fall to pieces" reflects a breakdown of the false ego and an awakening of an authentic self. It is a confusing and painful, but liberating, breakthrough into the heightened experience of O.

From this perspective, the "Fall" in the Garden of Eden, generally seen as a fall from God's grace, can be seen as a "fall" *into* grace, toward the god-like metaphysical knowledge. Bion (1977a) recognised the use or misuse to which such a fall or breakdown can be put, stating, "Many a façade has been saved by the misfortune that has made it a successful ruin" (p. 47). Implicit in this is the necessity of such a fall in order to crack the façade of a false self, but that merely patching up the cracks leaves a still workable but damaged façade without the potential for a genuine self capable of developing. These ruptures to the façade are opportunities to allow in feelings and thoughts which were excluded by the concrete fortress of the false self. In Leonard Cohen's (1992) song, "Anthem", he describes the valuable purpose of these cracks in our personalities as the means by which "light" can enter and illuminate the mind.

After partaking of the fruits of the Tree of Knowledge of Good and Evil and the Tree of Life, Adam and Eve fall from the unconscious bliss of ignorance into the possibility of consciousness. Once the "light" gets in, stripped of their blindness, vulnerable and confused, they notice they are different. They experience duality in the distinctions of male–female, good–evil, body–spirit, eternal–temporal, but these distinctions cannot yet be understood. These myths in Genesis describe the genesis of the mind and of consciousness, the integration of physical (carnal) and divine knowledge. As in the infant, this requires the development of thought, the journey toward consciousness on which Adam and Eve also now must painfully embark.

Humpty Dumpty's fragmentation reflects the infant's paranoid–schizoid position (Klein, 1946). For the *poet* Humpty Dumpty, however, or those adults in search of mental integration, this disorganised state of mind is a way station to a more evolved state now within their purview. Bion (1970) represents these adult fluctuating states of disorganisation and organisation as "Ps↔D", to distinguish them from the earlier primitive or pathological transitions of the paranoid–schizoid to the depressive position. He ascribes the mental function of "patience" to the chaos and uncertainty of the disorganised state which, if tolerated, can give rise to an integrated sense of "security" (p. 124). Grotstein (2007) describes Bion's new conceptualisation of Klein's theory as ". . . a higher dialectical dimension in which [the paranoid–schizoid and depressive positions] occur simultaneously and mediate one another" (p. 41).

This journey from disintegration to integration, from "patience to security" ends as the whole process begins all over again. Consciousness has no endpoint, it is an ongoing *process* in an infinite physical and mental universe. Once a question is answered, we are immediately faced with what we do not know. "The world of the unknown is before you: you are out in ultimate space . . . out in the mental stratosphere" (Bion, 1975, p. 27). The capacity to bear the uncertainty of the unknown and the sense of mental dis-integration it provokes is informed by a gradually growing background of experience and psychic development. This includes the capacity to tolerate frustration (patience), which allows for the mental containment of a thought (security).

Faith as a factor in thinking

Bion (1970) introduces the idea of "faith" as a function of patience, but it is a concept that differs essentially from traditional religious faith. For Bion, faith represents a belief in truth, and in one's capacity to tolerate the unknown as a means to truth. It is antithetical to the faith in an omnipotent and external God who provides answers to *alleviate* the frustrating mystery of the unknown. It is the difference between the *evasion* of frustration and the *modification* of frustration through thinking (ibid., p. 11). According to Freud's ideas about consciousness in "Formulations on the two principles of mental functioning" (1911b), the capacity to tolerate frustration implements the reality principle through secondary process thinking. Intolerance of frustration is the intolerance of reality, and so Bion's concept of faith includes the functions of reason and knowledge. Nietzsche makes a similar distinction, describing religious faith as the "acquired habituation to spiritual principles without reasons" (Nietzsche, 1882, p. 109, sec. 226).

For Bion (1970), faith is an experience of O with no association to memory or desire (p. 35). The suspension of memory, desire, and understanding requires an act of faith, a relinquishment of ego functions and immersion in the dimension of O, which opens the mind to essential truths. These are the "thoughts without a thinker", those stray or "wild" thoughts which, as Bion (1997) writes, ". . . you might try to domesticate" (p. 27). About these thoughts that evolve from contact with O, Bion says, "If entertained, they are conducive to mental health; if not, they initiate disturbance" (1970, p. 103).

In these terms, faith is a factor in mental health that can be understood to be inseparable from O. It facilitates knowledge, which develops empirically in the inherently paradoxical oscillations of primitive disintegration and integration. It might be compared to the fundamental duality in modern physics, as photons were discovered to act not only as particles, but also as waves. The idea of these antithetical yet simultaneous functions of light led to hypotheses about a fundamental unpredictability that was unsettling to physicists, most notably to Einstein (Hawking, 1988, p. 56). Although he was instrumental in these discoveries, Einstein found it difficult to accept the unpredictability of quantum theory. However, this paradoxical reality is similar, at least metaphorically, to the dilemma in the mind, where the intuitive and ultimately unknowable knowledge of dream-like oceanic waves co-exists with what might be called the "particularised" knowledge of the ego. The fundamental experience of duality is succinctly expressed by Beardsley (and Gray) (1904), who said, "I only melt to harden again" (p. 55), again indicating, like Bion's "Ps↔D", that the two states of mind oscillate in continuous and unpredictable ways. Poetry and art are created in the melted (intuitive) state of O; an analytic interpretation also forms in that melted state, but is fashioned into language and communicated to the patient with the help of that more organised, "particularised", or "harder" state of rational ego functioning. The creative mind, and mental health in general, is based on the ongoing dynamic *relationship* between these dual functions of the mind.

The Fall: clinical examples

The following session with Helen, the painter discussed in Chapter Three, demonstrates the painful journey toward knowledge as a process of trying to bridge the gap between the essential dualities of life and of the mind. This session took place about eight months later. As a reminder, Helen's traumatic childhood began with a premature birth, an emotionally detached mother and tyrannical father, and a violent older sister who often preyed on this sensitive little girl. Her means of mental survival was to lose herself in phantasy and imagination, which kept her isolated and detached from others and from her own feelings. After years of rage at me as a representation of her neglectful mother and abusive father, Helen's capacity for emotional contact with me increased, as did her conscious awareness of her feelings of terror. However, her responses to feelings are less likely now to be characterised by the anger and defensiveness we saw in the previous session.

Helen: Session 2

Helen began this end of the week session by saying, "*I can't remember all my dreams* but there were a lot of them."

> I remember rolling down a hill and then crawling back up, then rolling down again. I don't know if it was icy or I slipped but I kept rolling back down. There were big sculptures of Buddhas on the side. I accidentally knocked a piece off one of them and was crawling back up, maybe to fix it, but then rolled down the hill again. An animal had eaten all the flowers down to the nubs.

She said that the dream made her feel hopeless. She spoke of feeling discouraged by her new awareness of how she kept rejecting my help, terrified of letting anyone in. "I can't help doing it and maybe I never will." There was an animal burrowing under her garden in real life, she said, which ate some of the flowers, but not like in the dream. She talked about her friend, Katharine, whom she had just learnt from a friend was in treatment with an analyst I had recommended through another analyst. At that point there was some noise outside my office window and the patient said, "Is there a party out there or something?" I commented that apparently it sounded that way to her. (To my ears, however, it sounded like just a few people quietly talking and laughing.) She spoke of the constant noise and chaos in her childhood home, her sister's violence, and how she could never find a safe place.

I had the sense that Helen was somehow absent from the room. Her first statement, that she "couldn't remember all her dreams", had alerted me to some feelings of self attack, as if she were expected to remember them all but had fallen short. The idea that she somehow could, and should remember *all* her dreams was the kind of impossible expectation with which she often tortured herself. It reflected an oppressive superego that surely contributed to her hopelessness today. This primitive state of mind was also apparent to me in the dream and the rest of the session, for her reference to Katharine's analyst raised the issue of my outside life and her curiosity about what other patients or colleagues I was "partying" with when I was not with her. I thought the pain of our forthcoming weekend separation had contributed to her phantasied attempts to burrow into me (like the animal that had eaten all the flowers) to see what was going on—what kind of party (or sex) I was having, and to destroy any rivals. Her unbearable curiosity and the attendant feelings of separateness stimulated her desire to be inside of me like a foetus to avoid suffering the internal noise and chaos of her jealousy and need. However, this kept her imprisoned in that state of phantasy and imagination that she felt protected her. Despite her intelligence and sophistication in her outside life, and all the work she does to elevate herself (like climbing the hill in the dream), it is to these primitive feelings which Helen keeps unconsciously descending as she rolls back down the hill past the destruction of her internal life. In the figure of the Buddha, however, there also seemed to be some hope, and faith in her private mythology, in the tireless striving toward consciousness and enlightenment at the top of the hill. Like the broken Buddha, it is a damaged hope, I suppose, marred by unthought feelings of despair, anger, fear, and confusion. Still, she carries on, and I thought that the idea of these repeated descents to her primitive nightmares and ascents into the hope of mental development represented the organis-ing factor in the session.

Sisyphus and psychoanalytic meaning

Of course, this dream brought to mind the Greek myth of Sisyphus, condemned by the gods to repeat the meaningless and futile task of rolling a heavy stone to the top of the mountain, watching as it rolls back down, and then beginning the gruelling task again. I will put forward two different, seemingly contradictory interpretations of this myth. Both are true, however, depending on one's vertex. In fact, they are part of a whole, reflecting two levels of mental functioning. The first is the infantile level of the paranoid–schizoid and depressive positions in a mind not yet developmentally able to tolerate the frus-tration, a mind that is, unable to think. The second represents a more evolved level, the capacity to think, and the manifestations in adult-hood of the fluctuations between these two states (Ps↔D).

Like the myth, Helen's dream and her feeling of hopelessness seem, at first glance, to reflect the futility of existence. In his essay on the myth of Sisyphus, Camus (1955) notes that, for the ancients, noth-ing was more dreadful punishment than futile and hopeless labour. Camus sees the myth as the plight of man in modern industrialised society, a description of man's futile search for meaning in a world without God. It is a perspective also associated with existentialism and absurdist drama and literature, but, at the end of his essay, Camus does not find Sisyphus to be merely an absurd character destined to futile suffering. Sisyphus, he concludes, is, in fact, happy, for without God fate is a human matter. Being free of a punishing God (a primitive superego), "his fate belongs to him. His rock is his thing . . . The struggle itself is enough to fill a man's heart" (Camus, 1955, p. 91). The work, whatever it is, is not experienced as futile if it is truly one's work, that is, a fulfilment of the human destiny to develop the potential for consciousness.

We might reach the same conclusion from a psychoanalytic pers-pective, for this apparently futile struggle up and down the hill can be considered necessary steps in the journey toward being and the capacity to think. From this perspective, the patient's rock, "his thing", is his primitive concrete mind *capable* of development, but only through the knowledge gained in the repetitive climbs and falls of disintegration and integration in the analytic process. Through this process, one might begin to create a bridge between the two, between body and mind, between the primitive man and the awareness of the divine—O.

The happiness of any modern-day Sisyphus reflects an awareness of this process of growth and development. He is happy, that is, because of the ascents into an experience of the life of the self or mind, the experience of being that depends upon the descents to primitive mental states. Were this not so, it would be hard to explain why anyone would submit to the painful descents into primitive feelings in analytic work. The painful solitude of the journey, the existential loneliness, is the awareness of having a separate mind, but it is this that makes possible the development of mental potential, and imbues life with existential meaning. It is this, I think, which provides what Camus calls happiness, the fulfilment of the natural potential for a conscious mind which is the unique genetic heritage of the human animal.

The curiosity and the quest for knowledge depicted in the myths of Genesis are metaphorical depictions of the origins of consciousness, this inheritance of a mind capable of creative thought. The Fall in Eden and the fall of the tower of Babel which results in the confusion of tongues describe the obstructions to that dialectical journey to the divine knowledge which takes place through painstaking human effort. Bion delineates the difficulties this entails, pointing out that thinking does not develop automatically, but, rather, is something that must be learnt empirically by each infant, through the relationship with a mother who is herself capable of thinking. She must be capable, that is, of containing her own primitive mental states, in order to contain the infant's. While the *potential* for consciousness might be fundamental, natural, or "god-given", it is the work of the infant *in relation to* the mother who together can realise this divine potential.

This perspective supplants the idea of an external, all-knowing, punishing God with the idea of a human *process of learning* in the daunting task of mental evolution. Helen's work of fulfilling this potential is obstructed by her attachment to an external, punishing superego God, when, in fact, she is being punished by her own unknown feelings, long ago split off and projected. In such cases, Bion (1970) wrote, "Pain is sexualized; it is therefore inflicted or accepted, it is not suffered" (p. 19). This is in keeping with Klein's distinction between pain that is felt to be inflicted from without and one's own experience of mental pain.

Camus continues, "Sisyphus teaches the higher fidelity that negates the gods and raises rocks" (p. 91). Ultimately, what one transcends—through human effort and always intermittently—is the duality of reason divided from one's fundamental emotional self upon which reason is based, a resolution of a mind (spirit or soul) divided from the body. Both perspectives expressed in the myth of Sisyphus—of futility or hope—are, therefore, valid, it just depends on the level of mental development. Another way to put it is that the struggle up the hill, this rocky journey toward conscious thought, can be used in two different ways. Like Freud's repetition compulsion, it can lead to mindless repetition of the past due to the absence of a conscious mind able to think about its meaning, or to the resurrection of primal feelings of falling, disintegration, etc., which can be digested and integrated into the mind through the capacity to think. In the former, primitive state, the rock is experienced as a truly concrete "thing", a "beta element" incapable of use in thinking (Bion, 1962a). The analytic relationship is a process of helping the patient to tolerate the confusion and terror of the descents so that he or she can make use of the experience, a process of creating a mind able to contain feelings and to think.

Depending on the mental state in which one exists, the analysand's Sisyphean task is experienced either as a *sentence* of a living hell or a *process* of attaining "heaven". Sisyphus "happily" bears the burden of the rock as he rolls it up from those primitive depths to be viewed because of his hope of attaining the perspective of the higher ground of consciousness. There, at the top of the mountain, he achieves a moment of illumination and integration, followed by the inevitable return to the dis-integrated, primitive state of mind. However, if something is learnt, these descents into primitive mental states are less terrifying, for, while still emotionally and mentally challenging, they are informed by the earlier experiences of integration, and the increasing faith that the truth will again bring illumination and wholeness. The descents can then be experienced as transient, unlike the infant's experience, which lacks this perspective of time. As a result, these descents into unremembered "memories" can now be viewed not as fearsome harbingers of death, but as life, a fertile ground for growth. One can tolerate the "bad" feelings, in other words, knowing they are in fact "good", in the service of development.

For Helen, each inevitable descent returned her to the hellish hopelessness she encountered as a child. Again and again she *became* that infant dropped too early from her mother's womb, dropped after birth as well, with only an incubator to hold her, and then emotionally dropped in the absence of a sentient, conscious mother. There was a shift at some point in her analysis, after which these descents into primitive territories began to be experienced in the spirit of growth and learning. We will look at two more of her dreams in the next chapter on integration, but this next clinical example with "Fran" shows something of the dread of primitive feelings, and the development of the capacity to utilise the feelings into which she has fallen.

The fall contained: clinical vignette

"Fran" was a compulsive marijuana user when she began analysis eleven years ago. As long as one uses drugs, one can feel in control of the terrifying sensations of falling or being dropped into unmanageable unthinkable feelings, with no one there to stop one's fall. As Fran became sober, previously deadened emotions came to life and she isolated herself, retreating in fear, retreating from me emotionally as well. After several years of loneliness, hopelessness, and depression she is interested in being with people and has made new friends.

In this session she said, "I'm letting in more of life, but I'm terrified." She dreamt

> she was riding a horse at full speed toward a tall fence. She didn't know what to do, she was terrified she would not make it over the fence, but the horse jumped and they made it safely to the other side. She felt grateful to the horse and said, "Thank you, you're an amazing horse! Thank you for carrying me over such a high fence."

She associated horses with power. She then recalled an incident from age fourteen which was similar to the dream. Although she was an inexperienced rider, her grandfather had put her on a horse that was not fully tamed. Something spooked the horse, and it headed at full speed toward a fence, just as in the dream. Terrified, Fran shinned up his neck and slipped down, then let go and fell to the ground. Remarkably, she had escaped with just scrapes and bruises, but could not understand why her grandfather had put her in such danger. However, it reflected the general lack of safety she experienced growing up with a clinically depressed mother and a bombastic but emotionally absent father.

I thought that the power of the horse represented the uncontrollable It, or O, that untamed energy of her primal unconscious; it was a life force which, untamed, can be transformed into the force of death in the mind, overwhelming the self. When she was on drugs, and often promiscuous, what had often run away with her was that kind of uncontained energy based on detachment, mania, and fragmentation, that is, on mental "fission" rather than mental "fusion" (see above, p. 71). While this was experienced as a pleasurable high, it was followed by self-hatred, loneliness, and despair, for it was driven by a substitute for that primal force of life, her essential self. Addictions mimic the energy of the self, and so are often confused attempts to make contact with it, while, in fact, severing one's connection to the real thing. The real thing, like the horse, wild and untamed, is beyond one's control, while the drug, the effects of which one knows will end, appears to be reassuringly within one's control. Except, of course, one is addicted to emotional and mental death.

Real feelings from that primal place have a life of their own, and having begun to feel those uncontrollable feelings, Fran could, at times, tolerate the wild power of having an emotional life. As she gave up the illusion of control, her addiction to death was being slowly replaced by an "addiction" to life. She began relying more on other people and was enjoying herself, despite her feelings of terror. She was riding the "horse". In her memory about her grandfather, she had fallen off the horse, while this horse in her dream had helped to carry her, becoming a container for that uncontrollable force of emotional life. We might say that she had "remembered" this incident in her dream; after decades, she had finally been able to dream it. She was then able to use reason to think about these feelings. Her memory of having fallen revealed an idea of the fall as a good thing, as long as it was executed with some degree of control.

At the end of the session, Fran expressed gratitude to me for helping her over the years, and, from this perspective, I was the horse which had ferried her across the fence, in contrast to her grandfather, whose lack of emotional containment had led to a sense of falling all her life with no means of picking herself up. It was to this "grand" idealised internal father that she had clung all these years, to which she had been addicted. These feelings change, of course, practically in every session, as these addictions to life and death continue to be sorted out.

Towards the end of his essay on Sisyphus, Camus writes, "The boundless grief is too heavy to bear. These are our nights of Gethsemane. But crushing truths perish from being acknowledged" (Camus, 1955, p. 90). By way of example he says,

> Thus, Oedipus at the outset obeys fate without knowing it. But from the moment he knows, his tragedy begins . . .. Then a tremendous remark rings out: 'Despite so many ordeals, my advanced age and the nobility of my soul make me conclude that all is well'. (ibid.)

Conscious thought, even of the most painful and disturbing feelings, brings comfort and release, for, at the moment of knowing, faced with the full measure of one's humanness, of one's ignorance and mistakes, one is given the possibility of knowing one's self. Through the acceptance of one's own duality, one has the opportunity to develop the potential for truth, to have a mind. As Bion (1970) wrote, "The patient who will not suffer pain fails to 'suffer' pleasure and this denies the patient the encouragement he might otherwise receive from accidental or intrinsic relief" (p. 9).

CHAPTER NINE

Evolving states of wholeness and being

"a total stranger one black day
knocked living the hell out of me—
who found forgiveness hard because
my (as it happened) self he was
—but now that fiend and i are such
immortal friends the other's each"

(Cummings, 1950, p. 730)

Essential wholeness

Implicit in Bion's idea of an innate need for truth is the sense of something fundamentally whole in the personality, an inherently healthy mind that serves as the guardian of truth. In their theory of the aesthetic conflict, Meltzer and Harris express the view that wholeness is the infant's original state, concluding, in contradistinction to Klein's (1946) theory, that "the depressive position would be primary for development and the paranoid–schizoid secondary" (Meltzer & Williams, 1988, p. 28). They associate the notion of an innate, fundamental experience of wholeness with the infant's attraction to, and appreciation of, the beauty of the mother's breast.

However, they hypothesise that as the infant discovers himself to be separate from that beautiful mother, the baby recoils from this intense experience of beauty, ushering in splitting mechanisms to defend against the confusion of love and hate toward the mother. I would add to this the idea that emotional trauma in that early relationship is instrumental in that impulse to "recoil" from the mother (cf. Reiner, 2009a), although their point remains, that the divided self is *secondary* to an essential experience of wholeness.

The potential for wholeness and a sense of self resides in the infant's oceanic feeling, the primal experience of emotional truth. It is the infant's inchoate sense of being. However, it is important to recognise that this is only the *potential or precursor* to mental integration, which, as suggested, needs to meet with adequate conditions in order to develop into an evolved sense of being. The latter includes the capacity for continued mental growth, a development *toward* integration based on the incorporation of states of dis-integration. These fluctuating states of disjunction and wholeness, the paranoid–schizoid and depressive positions, cannot be neatly divided; rather, it seems that even the earliest version of *potential* wholeness includes a *simultaneous* experience of non-integration. As wholeness and division clash within the mind, the ensuing whirlpool of antithetical forces creates a fluidity of mental movement that mimics the infant's oceanic feeling.

The Hindu poem, *The Baghavadgita* (Bolle, 1979) presents a picture of the overwhelming nature of that experience of a fundamental self in contact with O. In Hindu terms, it is described as contact with the divine essence of an "imperishable" eternal essence, represented by the God, Krishna. In the beginning of the poem, that God essence is revealed to the warrior, Arjuna, as he stands paralysed at the prospect of an imminent battle with members of his own family. The young warrior is humbled before a terrifying vision of an infinite, awesome, all-encompassing Krishna, who is portrayed as "the entire world unified / Yet divided manifold, / Embodied in the God of gods" (ibid., p. 127: 13).

> Of many mouths and eyes,
> Of many arms, legs, feet,
> Many torsos, many terrible tusks . . .
> Ablaze with all the colors of the rainbow,

Touching the sky with gaping mouths and wide flaming eyes.
My heart in me is shaken.
O God, I have lost all certainty, all peace.

(ibid., p. 131: 23–24)

That fearsome experience of this infinite "God" is a description of O: infinite and all-encompassing, it is everything all at once. One opens to this all-inclusive vision with a mind equally inclusive, and so able to experience it in all its paradoxical unity and diversity. Arjuna's plight can be viewed analytically as the internal battle of separating his essential self from the primitive phantasies and introjections of his internal family, an experience of standing on his own in a state of being or mindfulness. It is experienced as an act of betrayal, however, against those aspects of the self identified with mother, father, etc. These internal objects need to be considered from the perspective Fairbairn (1952) raises, that objects are internalised because of deprivation and frustration, and their presence in the mind interferes with the dynamic wholeness of the mind. In the process of this birth into wholeness and emotional existence, the mask of a shrunken ego is overwhelmed by this larger vision of O, or "God", which recalls the primal emotional openness of infancy. This encounter with the incipient wholeness of an undeveloped, undivided neonatal mind returns one to the capacity to absorb the mother's awesome beauty ("God") as a whole spectrum of uncodified inner–outer sensations in one timeless instant. Arjuna describes aspects of this feeling. "I feel paralyzed, my mouth becomes dry, I tremble within, my hair stands on end . . . I cannot keep steady, my mind whirls" (Bolle, 1979, pp. 10–11).

This natural but fearsome oneness can be retrieved, as we see with Arjuna, if one dares to enter that state as an adult. Why one "chooses" to do this is mysterious. Why others do *not* do so is equally mysterious. On the one hand, the "reward" for one's curiosity is "a fearsome sense of disintegration, but, on the other hand, one feels a simultaneous sense of awe and oneness, a quintessence of life.

Despite all the lofty words used to define O—the infinite, eternal essence, absolute truth, ultimate reality, the godhead—none can adequately convey its aspect of religious awe as vividly as the poets. The following is E. E. Cummings' description of his first childhood encounter with what he called, "that mystery who is Nature" (1953, p. 32).

Here my enormous smallness entered her illimitable being, and possibly alive—someone who might almost (but not quite) have been myself—wonderingly wondered the mortally immortal complexities of Her beyond imagining imagination. (ibid.)

In his anthropomorphic depiction of Nature, Cummings conveys the infant's feeling of being lost in experience, surrendering control and rational understanding as one enters into this at-one-ment with the mother (or Mother Nature). Cummings' description shows the nuanced uncertainties and paradoxes as one flip-flops between opposing experiences, the truth of which lies somewhere in the middle. Of course, there is no "middle" in an infinite realm, and it is up to the reader to enter this non-linear realm, the oscillating dance between infinite and finite realities, in order to feel the dynamic internal movement of the mind's inherently paradoxical system. This constant movement is the dizziness Arjuna experiences as he steps away from the safe but constricting containment of the family, and which Paul (1997) points to as the state of mind of the patient moving from encapsulation to mental birth. Like Bion's idea about dreams that are present throughout waking life, this dance between opposing states is going on all the time, often beyond our awareness. It is no less real, however, than the unobservable fact of being on an Earth spinning on our own axis at over 1,000 miles per hour, and speeding around the sun at 67,000 miles per hour.

This mental dance is evoked in a poem by Arp, which shows the complex processes of a mind using language and thought to determine meaning. Again, like Arjuna's experience of Krishna, there is the sense of endless dizzying movement in this *mélange* of shifting sensual impressions, a circular sensation of a Moebius strip without beginning or end. Arp describes:

> . . . the echoes and the phrases
> and between the echoes and the phrases
> the reflections
> of echoes of mirrors.
>
> (Jean, 1974, p. xxxiii)

The state of oneness with experience is seen in the great musician who becomes one with the music, or the great writer or actor who loses his or her own personality in the character. It is in the process of becoming one with an object that the self is revealed, not in the object itself, but in the process of leaving the confinement of the shrunken ego and allowing the self to open into the larger mental realm represented by O. In this relationship of I–Thou, something is created beyond the two, something beyond the artist's control. De Kooning (1988) described how his work as a painter only felt interesting when he had a feeling of "slipping" or "falling", for only then did he get a "glimpse" (pp. 176–177), although he did not say of exactly what. In psychoanalytic terms it is O, a frighteningly intense glimpse of eternity in the temporary escape from the finite limits of the self.

This is implicit in Christ's enigmatic words to his disciples to renounce the self in order to follow God. "Anyone who finds his life will lose it; anyone who loses his life for my sake will find it" (Matthew 10: 39–40). Only in losing the mask of the false self does one find the self capable of metaphysical truth. There, one can *feel* one's existence, although, paradoxically, like the It, one does not live this self, one is lived *by* it as if it were something outside the self. The confusing nature of this idea is due in part to the fact that this multi-dimensional experience is bi-logical (Matte-Blanco, 1975) and non-linear in nature.

I first had experiences like these when I began painting in my late twenties. On one particularly clear Los Angeles day, for instance, everything seemed overwhelmingly, achingly vibrant, and as I looked at an imposing sycamore tree I sensed an animistic essence in its graceful growth toward the sky. I yearned for a way to express, not the beauty of the tree itself, but the *feeling* I had when looking at it, the *relationship* between us at that moment. My desire to paint it seemed to come from a simultaneous sense of being part of *and* separate from the experience. This state of oneness with the tree was similar to the infant's boundaryless relationship with the mother. It seems to me that even the fusion of infancy must also be informed by some kind of partial or proto-mental sense of separateness, a premonition of the mind. For one thing, the infant has already had the experience of birth, and for another, one cannot perceive something without some aspect of oneself to do the perceiving, even if it remains unconscious. It is analogous to Grotstein's (2000) exploration of the ineffable "dreamer who dreams the dream," who has no awareness of the origin of the dream and cannot claim authorship for it. In this case, I am talking about an inchoate infant with an incipient capacity to perceive the mother's beauty, and related to the essential knowledge of O. Although it seems antithetical to Winnicott's (1971) idea of there being no infant, just an infant–mother dyad, it does not seem to me to invalidate that idea, just to add to it the other side of the paradoxical equation, the infant's simultaneous proto-mental sense of being and connection, despite the lack of integrative functions.

I soon learnt that it was only when lost in that dream-like state that I could paint something which felt alive. I did not then have to try to make the painting alive, I simply had to *be* in that state, which was automatically reflected in the image on the canvas. Of course, it is not really so simple, for it is equivalent to the analyst's discipline of eschewing memory, desire, and understanding, to become one with an unseen essence in the patient. This helps bring life to his interpretation so that it has the power to bring truth and life to the patient's mind. It is a non-psychotic experience of dis-integration, for it includes the integration of one's connection to the object (or, in this case, the tree).

While some might find it occultist to talk about animistic spirits in trees, this vital energy is not attributed to gods or supernatural beings, but to that natural level of the supernatural delineated by Bion (above p. 59). It is analogous to the sub-atomic level of matter where it is interchangeable with energy, where seemingly separate and inanimate material objects are engaged in an invisible dance of shared, interacting energy. The fact that we cannot physically see or otherwise sensually experience these things, either at the deepest level of matter or the deepest levels of the mind, does not mean they do not exist. As Freud (1893f) often quoted Charcot as saying, "*La théorie, c'est bon, mais ca n'empêche pas d'exister*" ("Theory is good, but it doesn't stop things from existing" (p. 13). Charcot's idea reflects the realm of O, the truth of a world that exists despite what we are able to think.

My own creative experiences were ushered in by a terrifying descent into a feeling of boundless uncertainty. With the benefit of an analyst who could recognise this sense of treading at the edge of madness as an opportunity to open into a more expansive self, I was able to put these experiences to good use. There was great relief in being able to use such challenging emotional experiences to give form to an experience of boundarylessness. It resulted in a feeling of integration, as the sense of dis-integration was tempered by being contained and expressed in the creation of something new. One then no longer feels lost in that infinite oceanic world, nor does one feel the need anxiously and prematurely to impose a structure to bind that unbound mental freedom before it can reveal its essential meaning. It exemplifies the co-operation between container and contained that Bion (1970) calls a commensal relationship "in which two objects share a third to the advantage of all three" (p. 95). The emotional experience could be sufficiently contained by the "languages" of shape, colour, and composition to produce the third, more mysterious, object of a painting. In the process, primitive fears of fragmentation are ameliorated by the faith that one will be held by the meaningful expression of the experience. From this perspective it is also an example of the adult journey of Ps↔D, the patience to tolerate the disorganised feelings which lead to a moment of the security of containment, knowledge, and integration.

This relationship is at the heart of Bion's (1970) description of genius as a capacity to use one's psychotic mechanisms in the service of life and growth. From this standpoint, genius is not a judgement—either positive or negative—on the value of that which is created, it is a description of this mental process. Artists or writers are often blocked by tendencies to judge their own work by superficial or conventional standards, but, from this perspective, a work of art gains merit by its ability to satisfy the criterion Bion put forth, to use psychotic mechanisms in the service of life and growth.

Since opposing poles cannot be clearly divided, determining what is or is not in the service of life is not always clear. Clinically, this is a tricky issue, for in assessing that fine and very blurry line, the analyst must be careful not to obstruct the patient's often weak and easily inhibited force of life. Helen, for instance (see the "Sisyphus" dream, above, p. 113), was a gifted painter, but having relied on phantasy and imagination to escape destructive feelings toward her hostile and chaotic family, she had developed a kind of hypertrophied imagination which kept her isolated from others and from her emotional life. Her creative work was successful and critically acclaimed, but, since it carried this unconscious defensive intention, she often had difficulty appreciating her work. What others saw as beautiful paintings, in her eyes were tainted by that early unconscious hatred toward her parents. The split from those old feelings was such that unconsciously she did not even recognise her work as her own. In this case, the sense of emptiness or non-being necessary to creative work was not contained within a relationship to her conscious self and left her empty of energy and ideas.

All creative work is an incalculable combination of aggressive and libidinal forces, but in Helen's case the balance kept being tipped by these unconscious defences against her aggression. She would then be overtaken by self-hatred, guilt, and confusion. This can become the source of serious artistic blocks, but awareness of the unconscious feelings that kept Helen imprisoned in the past enabled her to continue working and increasingly to appreciate her work.

Suspension of memory and desire: "the cloud of unknowing"

In *Memoir of the Future*, Bion's dream-like "autobiography" of his inner life, he claimed to have been dogged and imprisoned all his life by commonsense, and by memories and desires and understanding. These experiences of an imprisoning ego surely informed Bion's awareness of the importance of eschewing memory, desire, and understanding in order to be released from the imprisoning ego which blocks creativity. In speaking of the suspension of memory and desire, Bion's (1970) ironic quip, "A bad memory is not enough" (p. 41), underlines the idea that suspending memory and desire in contact with O is not simply a return to the infant's state of mind. Like the mystic's cloud of unknowing, it is the discipline and emotional containment of the adult mind which enables one to revisit that primitive state with a mind now able to symbolise them in dreams and thought.

The mask of the ego as superego

The crippling commonsense ego Bion described really functions as a primitive superego. The degree of fear and resistance at the prospect of leaving this imprisoning–imprisoned self is directly related to the degree to which that pathological and punishing superego is aligned with the ego. The Freudian superego (1923b) measures the ego against an ideal formed of the child's need to please the parent. It is not directed by a fundamental aspect of the self that, in its original wholeness, has access to natural truths of good and bad. Freud's notion of the ego ideal seems to reflect an idealised self needed to defend against unconscious negative feelings toward the object. The idealised self, identified with the god-like parent, becomes an internal object dominated by a severe split and, therefore, antagonistic to these basic truths. It is closer to what Bion (1962a) calls a "super-ego" (p. 98) that is moralistic but has no morality, dominated by envy, violence, and hatred of truth. Its harsh judgements are not informed by reason and thought, it is materialistic and anti-scientific, it cannot think, for thinking would require the individual to feel the dangerous negative thoughts he or she is trying to keep at bay. This "super-ego" reflects a corrupted version of the natural potential for conscience and morality based on inherent wholeness and the desire for truth. What remains of that natural potential for a conscience is the imprisoning and crippling ego–superego, incapable of developing a mature moral ethos (cf. Reiner, 2009b).

In this next clinical example, we see that the "fall" from that lofty god-like ideal to a place of flawed and painful humanness might be so precipitous that the patient clings ferociously to that identification with a god-like and wrathful superego which forbids knowledge of feelings.

"Robert": Session 1

"Robert", a sensitive and intelligent man, was one of four siblings who grew up with a verbally abusive schizophrenic mother and an emotionally withdrawn father, who divorced when Robert was twelve. Insecure, depressed, and withdrawn, he often hid in his room to escape his mother's violent outbursts. The despair of this inhospitable emotional environment led to his phantasy that he had the power to cure his mother. Bright, likeable, and ambitious, Robert became a doctor during his first ten years of analysis, despite bouts of morbid anxiety. In this session, he described his disappointment at having failed to get a teaching position he had expected. He felt worthless, unloved, and wanted to die. He dreamt:

> I was working at a new office, there were tons of patients there and interns to teach. I was trying to manage everyone and felt *excited* that people

wanted my help but I also felt *overwhelmed* . . . so I was discouraged too, in total despair.

Robert could not figure out why he felt so bad, since in reality things in his life were going well—he had a successful practice that he enjoyed, a loving wife, and a new paper just published. As in the dream, he was excited about his work but felt crippled by despair. I saw this combination of excitement and being overwhelmed as the core of the session, a reflection of the feelings he had in his early attempts to save his mother. While overwhelmed by the task, his delusion that he could save her was exciting, but his realisation that he could not left him overwhelmed again by anxiety and failure. Accepting this failure to cure her meant he was not a God, just a helpless, unhappy little boy. In an effort to convince himself of his superpowers, he had even managed to become a doctor, but none of it changed the reality of that sad and terrified little boy who lacked a mother to take care of him. His "new office" now was that old "office" of his delusory healing powers over his first patient, his mother. Nothing he did as a real doctor could match that omnipotent God/ self, although this God, being just a little boy's phantasy, could not actually cure anyone at all. He gave no credit to the human doctor he had worked so hard to become, who *was* helping people, but who, compared to that idealised God, had no meaning. Averse to feelings and to thinking, and meant to protect him from the pain of having no mother, this superego God also kept him unable to grow into the man whose life he was living like a shadow. Despite having been recognised as a competent and caring doctor, he often felt insecure about his work and himself, for that adult self had no existence in his mind.

As I interpreted some of this to Robert, I could sense his despair in the painful realisation that his continued efforts to cure his mother were delusions, evidence for which we can see in the next session.

"Robert": Session 2

Robert felt depressed, and "annoyed with everyone". He had no patience to listen to his patients' problems, a complaint I had never heard him express. He dreamt:

> I was in my old friend, Bella's, bathroom, it was all white. I noticed an abscess on my leg and tried to drain it, and a huge amount of pus and blood oozed out, it got all over the rug. It really hurt, but I knew the blood would stain and I didn't know if I should clean it up or finish draining the wound. I thought Bella would be mad but I kept draining the wound. I thought, at least I got the infection out.

He said that Bella, a friend and massage therapist, had been depressed and in bad financial straits. However, she was now doing well, having obtained "an amazing great job" as a personal massage therapist to a wealthy businesswoman. Robert said he had, in fact, got blood on his own rug after cutting his toe. I thought this important clue was the selected fact. Bella and her "great job" were then linked to himself, and I thought that he, like Bella, had been a kind of "massage therapist" for his mother, massaging her mental pains, her ego, so to speak, pacifying her in the vain hope of assuaging her illness. His anger, depression, and confusion were hidden behind the mask of that helpful little boy. In this context, today's depression and his annoyance at his patients seemed like a positive shift, for these feelings were more in line with his real self, finally having a real reaction to his first patient, his mother. The "great job" which had saved him from depression in infancy and childhood was the primitive delusion that he was the "doctor/mother" who could cure his mother. What he did not know is that his "amazing job" kept him from doing his real job of becoming himself.

This dream was also significant in terms of the transference. I pointed out that in his dream he had got the infection out, by which I thought he meant that it was out in the open in his mind and in the treatment. However, since the process of cleaning it out is so painful, he is also irritated with me, for as these messy, pus-y feelings of despair and anger at his mother emerge, I am felt to be that mother who cannot contain them. However, he is also angry with me as me, his analyst, who, he rightly feels, is tainting that pure "white" image of his helpful Bella self, revealing it to be a sham.

Robert was quiet. He admitted that he did feel angry with me, for he did not feel capable of giving up these old beliefs that made him feel powerful and special. His guilt about hating his mother also became apparent as he thought that he must have done something terribly wrong to deserve her wrath. He was unsure if I was the crazy mother, filling him with more poison, or a good mother/analyst who might help him clean out the infection from his long-growing mental abscess. These two views of me as good and bad mother–analyst are at this point entangled in his mind.

The climb toward unity

Robert's suspicions of me had been growing in the last year, but he now became more clearly engaged in the struggle of distinguishing the two aspects of himself. I felt that he was on that very rocky path of a psychological/spiritual climb to his own sense of being, for he had become aware of the part of *him* that undermines his accomplishments and his self. The metaphor of the climb up the mountain toward this "elevated" state of consciousness is a common one. Moses (Exodus 19: 3) went alone to the top of Sinai and found the divine wisdom of God. The Tower of Babel (Genesis 11: 4) and the "confusion of tongues" is another version of this upward climb toward divine knowledge of the higher mind, as well as the inevitable fall into confusion and fragmentation. What is forbidden in Babel is communicative language, without which one lacks the means to develop higher conceptual thought.

We might conjecture about a physiological basis to this upward drive, perhaps a vestige of primal knowledge of the developmental ascent from the primitive functions of the basal ganglia—or "reptile brain"—into the neocortex, the centre of higher mental functions of language, learning, memory, and conscious complex thought. Over the years, some of my patients' dreams have suggested this connection, for, as their capacities to experience their primitive feelings increased, I saw versions of Herculean struggles to hoist themselves up. There were images of an urgent need to lift the whole weight of their bodies up over the precipice of a mountain. Robert, too, had several dreams in which he struggled to pull himself up out of the water and on to a pier. These particular patients had in common the traumatic physical or emotional absence of a parent to help them contain their feelings, but I also saw in them what Bion (1992) called a constitutional "disposition to truth" (p. 262). This seemed to provide an impetus, and the wherewithal, to endure catastrophic changes in their personalities, an inclination not shared by everyone. I further noticed in these people that their efforts in dreams of this kind were, at first, usually alone. As the work progressed, there was sometimes someone at the top of the mountain helping them up, or on the dock pulling them from the water, like a proto-mental awareness of an analyst/obstetrician helping them to be born.

In *Thus Spoke Zarathustra* (1885a), Nietzsche's Zarathustra is also transformed by his climb to the top of the mountain, a lonely journey in which he communed only with the animals of the forest. Zarathustra describes the elevated man, the *Übermensch*, as a bridge between man's animal nature and his reason. It is not seen as a fixed mental structure, but as a *process* of learning to tolerate these conflicting aspects of the self, an ongoing negotiation between inner life and outer experience. Nietzsche (1885a) described it as "a bridge, not a goal" (p. 44).

Zarathustra, like Moses, descends from the mountain in order to impart this knowledge to the people. On his way, he meets a sage who notices that Zarathustra has become "a child, an awakened-one" (ibid., p. 40). The sage asks why he wants to return to "the sleepers", and Zarathustra replies that his love of mankind demands that he return to give them this gift of knowledge. Nietzsche certainly shared the awareness, like Cassandra, that the people did not want this knowledge. He believed that his idea of an integrated man was before its time, a mental development that would have to wait to be realised by the evolution of an *Übermensch*, a free and elevated thinker, what Bion (1970) describes as the "exceptional individual", the genius", or "mystic" (p. 64).

For Bion, the bridge exists in the relationship between Ps↔D. This is a function of container and contained, which he described as, "perhaps the most important mechanism employed by the practising psychoanalyst" (Bion, 1970, p. 123). Through states of reverie, in that primitive cloud of unknowing, the analyst's focus shifts from what is already known and so at the moment irrelevant (K), to the unknown and unknowable (O), which allows for oneness with the patient at a metaphysical level. We can see here the concordance of all these theories—container and contained, the fluctuations of Ps↔D, the suspension of memory and desire, reverie—all united by the state of mind of O.

William Blake's (1790) romantic and, at the time, revolutionary poem, *Marriage of Heaven and Hell*, eloquently expresses the primacy of the bridge which effects an experience of wholeness and being. He describes the 'Errors' of the dualistic view of religion, with its sharply divided opposites of good and evil.

> Attraction and Repulsion, Reason and Energy, Love and Hate . . .
> From these Contraries spring what the religious call Good and Evil.
> Good is the passive that obeys Reason, Evil is the active springing
> from Energy.
>
> Good is Heaven. Evil is Hell. (p. 413)

From that perspective, the disembodied soul is felt to be pure and good, and the body, with its irrevocable needs and passions, is felt to be evil. Blake concludes, however, that the body and soul are one, a unified state of mind beyond the dichotomy of good and evil. These dualities cannot be separated. Bion makes the same point regarding the relationship between states of omnipotence and helplessness, "There can be no single word that can describe one thing without also describing its reciprocal" (Bion, 1992, p. 370).

Blake goes on to say:

> . . . That called Body is a portion of the Soul,

> Energy is the only life and is from the Body and Reason is the bounds.
> . . . [the] circumference of Energy. Energy is Eternal Delight. (1790,
> p. 413)

Blake makes it clear that Energy (like the uncontrollable forces of O, the It, the id) is not evil, neither is it at odds with reason; it is *contained within* reason by thought. But these "marriages" are uneasy resolutions of the duality at the core of life. There is no end or lasting peace, since furthering one's knowledge in an infinite world demands that one continue to revisit the unknown, unbounded, dis-integrated energy of life—the womb of knowledge and creativity.

Mental wholeness, a clinical vignette

Helen: Session 3

The development of a sense of being and wholeness are illustrated in these two consecutive sessions with Helen, which took place six months after the "Sisyphus" dream (above, p. 113). At that point, every interpretation felt to her like a traumatic fall from the false security of a deadened self into the primitive states of mind she felt to be so brutalising.

Helen spoke about her current art exhibit, which had been well received. She felt proud of the work, which she thought was more emotionally revealing. Since she generally judged herself so harshly, this was unusual for her, and it seemed to confuse her. She was awakened by the following dream in the middle of the night, feeling bereft.

> *My mother was moving*, either because she sold her house or she was dying. I woke myself up crying, "Mummy, mummy, I want my mummy!"

I thought that Helen's new emotional openness had frightened her, so that it was she who was "moving" out of "her mother's house", that internal refuge from her emotional life. As she stepped into her real self she felt unmoored, a psychological birth that carried with it the terror and despair of her actual birth, the premature separation from her mother's womb at birth. She feared then that her mother had died, as she now fears the death of this phantasied womb mother into whom she retreated. Although this imprisons and isolates her, she fears reality as well, being imprisoned by the limitations of life and reality with no defensive refuge from her feelings.

I interpreted her terror that if she makes progress, I, like her mother, will throw her out prematurely, end the analysis before she is ready. As painful as this was, she was able to recognise this terrifying "fall" into that early trauma as a move into her life, that long-hidden self from which she had been exiled. In the wake of this nascent capacity to think about the meaning of her fall, we can see Helen begin the upward climb in a different way in the next day's dream.

Helen: Session 4

> I was in a house with Ian (an ex-boyfriend). I'd come to collect some belongings I'd left behind, but I had no interest in seeing him. I went to a room and had to climb a very steep ladder to the top of some bookshelves. I found a drawing up there that I'd done as a child, signed just like I used to sign my name . . . I was so happy to have it, it was something I wouldn't have wanted to lose.

She said that Ian had rejected her in a cruel way, adding, "I wish I hadn't wasted my time on men like that, but I just didn't know myself then." She talked for a while about how she loved doing artwork as a child. In thinking about her dream, I was struck by the fact that this time Helen's climb did not result in a fall. On the contrary, the drawing she finds at "the top" is evidence of a capacity to symbolise the pain of her childhood. Having "fallen" into infancy in the last session had resulted in the capacity to *think about* the fall in this one, to dream it, and so be lifted up. Yesterday's primal fear and yearning for her mother was here transformed by being contained in that dreaming function, for she now discovers something of value from her childhood. She makes the critical distinction between her painful experiences with her cruel father (Ian) and the value of going back there to feel and think about those experiences. At the "top", the capacity for dreaming—the images of her drawing—facilitates a moment of consciousness (or alpha function), and her capacity to *think about* the trauma. We see her awareness of the value of that primitive self—her "name" or primal identity—with which she feels she cannot afford to lose contact.

When good is bad

In this context, Nietzsche's (1886) idea about the state of mind "beyond good and evil" warrants more detailed discussion. The challenges of integration in Helen's nascent ascent to her mind is germane to the fundamental confusion between good and bad we regularly see at primitive levels of the personality. According to Nietzsche, efforts to distinguish good from bad cannot be determined merely by socially accepted conventions or religious values. The more essential values and meanings have to be determined not by one's actions, but by the intentions *behind* one's actions. This revolutionary challenge would require a "free thinker" (p. 55, par. 4), a new way of thinking with a new kind of mind to think it. Clearly, this also refers to Nietzsche himself. The freedom and uniqueness of his thinking is reflected in his often non-linear thought processes and the passion of his writing, which seem to be direct emanations from this primitive realm. A free thinker, in his view, is someone able to reassess the conventional values embedded in one's mind through the language and ethos of the culture.

Our highest insights must—and should—sound like follies and sometimes like crimes when they are heard . . . by those who are not predis-
posed and predestined for them . . . What serves the higher type of
men as nourishment or delectation must almost be poison for a very
different and inferior type. (Nietzsche, 1886, p. 42)

The challenge of sorting out these conflicting impressions of good
and bad was exemplified in Helen's capacity to see the good in the
bad feelings. Robert, too, began to see his feelings of hatred toward his
mother not just as poison to be feared and discarded, but as valuable
aspects of his emotional life which needed to come to awareness, to
be "expressed", like the pus-filled abscess in need of being drained.
Related to this, his suspicions about the bad me who was the stimu-
lus for this painful awareness could only be sorted out by recognising
the value of these "poisonous" feelings. All of this meant challenging
the traditional values of the seemingly "loving" good boy upon which
his entire moral system had been based, the perfect selfless self (the
pristine white rug), which had, in fact, been a cruel attack on his mind
that left him without a self. Only the thinker free of conventional
views of good and bad can see the destructiveness in "goodness" and
the positive value of "destructiveness".

Bion (1970) mentions the idea of an interpretation which is "death
to the existing state of mind" (p. 79). His bold statement below would
be at home in the pages of Nietzsche's *Beyond Good and Evil*.

In psycho-analysis it is assumed that a theory is false if it does not seem
to minister to the 'good' of the majority of mankind. And it is a
commonplace idea of good. The whole idea of 'cure', of therapeutic
activity, remains unscrutinized . . . Too much of the thinking about
psycho-analysis precludes the possibility of regarding as good a theory
that would destroy the individual or the group. Yet there will never be
a scientific scrutiny of analytic theories until it includes critical
appraisal of a theory that by its very soundness could lead to a destruction of mental stability, e.g. a theory that increased memory and desire
to a point where they rendered sanity impossible. (Bion, 1992, p. 378)

What if a "good" or truthful interpretation destroys the patient's
stability, an outcome conventionally felt to be "bad"? The analyst is
regularly faced with just such a dilemma. Truth and lies (life and
death, good and bad) are mistaken for each other, and we further find
that patients often prefer the lie. "The patient, especially if intelligent

and sophisticated, offers every inducement to bring the analyst to acceptance of the lie as a working principle of superior efficacy" (Bion, 1970, p. 99). The patient might be horrified to hear that he prefers to continue poisoning his mind with untruths rather than bear the pain of change. While this might be due to envy or perversion, it could be due to the confusion at that primitive level, that what is bad or poisonous has been defined as good. Because Robert's "lies" had protected him from the onslaught of truths he was incapable of tolerating as a baby, they were indeed "good" at the time, but they are now part of a primal confusion which obstructs thinking and emotional development.

Religious notions of morality need to be reassessed with reference to these ideas about the fluidity of values. The basis of the fifth commandment, for instance—"Honour thy father and thy mother"—can be seen as instinctual. It is useful from a survival standpoint, since parental love is of fundamental importance in the infant's attachment to the mother. However, if the infant's hatred is stimulated by a real-istically neglectful or disturbed mother, the child's innate need for love and attachment can become pathological. The child is presented with a moral dilemma (Fairbairn, 1940). Does he choose the general truth of the fifth commandment, which, in this case, has become a lie, or does he choose his own truth determined by his own experience? This choice is not really available to the infant who has not yet devel-oped the capacity to think. But it is the real extenuating circumstances that force him to deny the more primal instinct of attachment, even though denying his experience means replacing truth with the mask of a loving self. In this case, the feeling of love is a lie. These confu-sions between love and hate, between truth and lies, become tena-ciously rooted in the personality and obstruct the development of the self. For the infant whose mind is, as yet, incapable of sorting out this moral dilemma, the lie is preferable to hating a mother upon whom one depends for one's survival. Still, protecting his love for the parent can be seen as evil, though it is predicated on behaviour which is loving and so ostensibly "good".

The idea that there are exceptions to these religious laws is also implicit in this message in the New Testament.

"I have come not to bring peace to the world, but a sword. I have come to set a man against his father, a daughter against her mother . . . a man's enemies will be those of his own household. (Matthew 10: 24–26)

If those of one's family are not interested in fundamental truths, one is compelled by one's own primal need for truth to break the commandment. Like Arjuna, one must take up arms against one's family (above, pp. 123–124). The further complication, of course, is that, according to object relations theory, one's "own household" also represents the relationships within one's mind, those internal objects against whom one must wage war if one is to uphold one's essential truth.

Free will

What becomes inexorably confused is the distinction between a moral imperative approved by the majority or group and the individual's responsibility to determine truth based on his own, always idiosyncratic, experience. Without the capacity to think, one is not equipped to distinguish the two. It reflects the distinction between free will, in which the individual has a say in his own fate based on his experience, and the divine will of a primitive God, in whose hands the individual's fate is already felt to be sealed.

"God is dead"

Nietzsche often railed against the hypocrisy of Christian values, not because its laws are immoral, but because they *become* immoral if universally imposed and obeyed rigidly—one might say "religiously"—rather than through the exercise of reason. These values become sterile and meaningless, as they are divorced from the mental intercourse between emotion and reason. It is this sterile, mindless version of Christianity about which Nietzsche (1882) famously proclaimed, "God is dead" (p. 181), a statement often seen as nihilistic but which, in fact, appears as a lament delivered by a madman in *Thus Spoke Zarathustra*. Again, Nietzsche is, no doubt, alluding to himself, knowing that these complex and challenging ideas would seem to conventional society like the rantings of a madman. He declares that it is man who has killed the holy God with pious pretentions which mask less acceptable underlying intentions. The lies and partial truths which masquerade as piety have destroyed true morality and true religious feeling, which can be determined only in the specific emotional context of the individual.

The analyst's job is to uncover these lies and communicate something of the meaning and intentions of the patient's beliefs. This can restore that "God" within, that aspect of the self with access to the freedom of thought of that metaphysical realm of knowledge. The analyst's thinking has to be sufficiently free to recognise as "bad" something that is apparently "good", or vice versa. In Robert's dream (above, p. 131), his happiness for his friend's "amazing job" led me at first to think of it as a good thing and, by extension, as representing something positive on an intrapsychic level. As Bion (1970) points out, however, O is "a non-human system" (p. 103), and the analyst must think beyond personal and conventional assumptions, beyond good and evil, memory and desire, in order to hear that which is not obvious in that other unsaturated system of new thoughts. The truths of that infinite realm are easily lost early on in the convulsive maelstrom of primitive experience.

Emptiness: a space for being

The mind exists as empty space. In a sense, it is like outer space, which has no existence in itself but which forms the background necessary to the existence of everything that is contained within it, the matter and dark matter of stars and planets and all the forces which link them together or repel them from each other. In the case of the inner space of the mind, however, it is not enough merely to have this empty space; one must also *experience* it consciously. Paradoxically, one's sense of existence depends upon his or her awareness of this non-existent empty space within.

One patient, for instance, constantly complained of how busy he was, how his law firm was depleting him, leaving him stressed, with no time for himself. As it turned out, that was precisely what he liked about it, for when he finally took a day off, he did not know what to do with himself, he could not stand the feeling of space. This was a man who had detached himself from his seductive mother as a child. It gave him a feeling of power over his confused feelings of instinctual attraction and emotional repulsion from his mother's primitive projections. However, this "solution" left him detached from himself as well, for he had collapsed the space in his mind in which his feelings might have been contained. What was left was a negative space filled with "lies", a kind of anti-mind, inhospitable to truth, with no potential for something real to develop there. Jason often filled the session with irrelevant chatter unconsciously meant to hide the truth. Although he practiced Yoga and had devoted himself to finding his whole essential self, his unconscious aim was to remain fragmented in order to avoid feeling his terrifying emptiness and confusion. Unconsciously, he was working hard to render me irrelevant, as he had done with his mother, all the while hiding, or killing, that terrified motherless boy.

What this patient could not tolerate was any space between us in which he might have felt his need for me. According to Bion's (1970) concept of "the no-thing", the awareness of the mother's absence creates a mental space for a thought—the thought, "no breast", or "no mother", or "no-thing" (p. 35). For a child too early faced with loss or confused intentions toward the mother, that space becomes annihilated. There is no space for mental reality, for that internal playground of feeling, thought, passion, and existence. Bion writes, "There is thus created a domain of the non-existent" (p. 20). This now non-existent space is that anti-mind filled with terrifying fragments of the self; it becomes terror itself without any human aspects.

The "miracle" of the Virgin birth provides a symbol through which we can think about that space ushered in by the capacity to tolerate the mother's absence. Such a "miracle", untenable by rational standards, metaphorically represents that empty space in which something new mysteriously forms. Like O and Bion's eschewal of memory and desire and understanding, this mental womb becomes the container from which is born an *idea* that appears to come from nowhere, nowhere earthly, that is, for it is the creative mental fruit of a transcendent "God" consciousness. It is a thought, apparently without a thinker. What is created is not the literal baby Jesus, the child of God without an earthly father, but the mental "child" of one's contact with O, the gnostic representation of Christ as truth and the spiritual functioning of the bi-modal mind. It is created through contact with the "divine" state of mind of the mystic's empty cloud of unknowing—O. This "virgin birth" is born of that painful emptiness each time one allows the space for a question to remain unanswered and a new thought to be dreamt.

CHAPTER TEN

Summary and conclusions

> "Be patient toward all that is unsolved in your heart and try to love the questions themselves . . . Do not now seek the answers, which cannot be given you because you would not be able to live them . . . Live the questions now"
>
> (Rilke, 1934[1902], p. 35)

I n religious terms, O refers to "God", or the spirit, or the soul; in Hindu philosophy, it is the imperishable eternal essence, and in Rilke's terms, the "angelic order"; for Kant, it is the "thing-in-itself", and for Plato, "pure Forms". Despite the impossibility accurately to represent in words this ephemeral essential level of truth, I have tried to show the necessity of access to this metaphysical realm for the development, health, and, ultimately, the survival of the mind.

Bion locates the source of our capacity for contact with the ultimate reality of O in the infant's inherent capacity and need for truth. Winnicott's (1971) description of the infant's relationship of oneness with the mother seems to me to require the additional understanding of an infant who, *at the same time*, is already capable of an experience of itself, albeit a proto-mental experience of wholeness, preliminary to mindful integration. As yet undeveloped and incapable of being mentally represented, this mind/self exists as potential in a primal but sentient state, a premonition or "pre-conception" (Bion, 1962b, p. 111) of consciousness. Precursors to this idea can be found in Fairbairn's ideas about endopsychic structure and his view of the infant as an "initially integrated but undifferentiated self" (Scharff & Birtles, 1994, p. xv).

The paradoxical reality of a neonatal infant who experiences both separateness and oneness reflects the multi-dimensional sensations, the *everything-all-at-once* described in *The Baghavadgita* as "the imperishable eternal essence" (above, p. 143). It is found in the infant's innate oneness with feeling states, the capacity for contact with its own emotional reality—O. This does not mean that the infant *knows* himself, or knows even that it is his own emotional reality he is experiencing. Rather, that in that oneness with his own *experience* this premonition, or preconception, of selfhood and consciousness exists. Like the innate preconception of the breast which Bion described, there is an innate preconception of these states of mind which are part of the heritage of human mental development.

We might say that in this *pre*conception of a self there is a self already in the process of being conceived, a self that is "pending", or held in abeyance until it can be realised through the relationship with another sentient being. In the absence of such a person, the infant in that proto-mental phase is, in a sense, *Waiting for Godot*, a seemingly timeless wait in an infinite universe for someone who might or might not make sense of these truths he does not *know* but which, inherently, he *is*, and which he instinctually yearns to have developed through his capacity to think.

As we have seen, the infant's "unknowing knowing" differs from the adult's conscious sense of being, or selfhood, or becoming, although they both derive from the same source. For the adult, relinquishing the limited self of an ego driven by sensory existence might allow a glimpse of the experience of the godhead, which Grotstein (2007) calls "godhood" (p. 43n). It is a self in contact with the other non-sensual realm of knowledge derived from an experience of O.

We are used to thinking of the self as a stable entity, but even the adult experience of a knowing self once again quickly becomes unknown in the transient fluctuations of Ps↔D. The challenge of these ideas is the acceptance of one's own self as constantly changing and unpredictable, a self, that is, unknown to one's self. Like the Hassayampa River, which disappears underground then reappears once more, that more expansive self keeps being lost to oneself. Para-doxically, it is when one allows oneself to be lost as well, to suspend access to the sensuous world, that one can know oneself best. Immersed in that metaphysical reality, one's thoughts are directed by the "It", or O, and so even one's own thoughts, born of that collabo-ration with the unknown, are unknowable from the standpoint of linear thought. As Browning said, "Once only God and Robert Brown-ing knew what [this poem] meant, now only God knows" (Welles, Bogdanovich, & Rosenbaum, 1998). In that poetic "trance", or the hallucinosis of O, one may not know in linear terms even what one is saying himself.

Since even one's own thoughts present these difficulties in comprehension, Bion's (1975) remark about scientific meeting is not surprising, "We often talk in a way which sounds exactly as if we talked the same language. It is very doubtful" (p. 23). The difficulty of describing verbally anything of this numinous realm should be obvi-ous by now, and I must say that I am always impressed by, and grate-ful for, the experience of having understood anything at all of this intangible, ephemeral realm. The consequences for psychoanalysis, which relies on verbal intercourse, are obvious. While painting, or poetry, or fiction might seem more understandably drawn from that non-linear realm of the mind, psychoanalytic insight, or any creative new ideas, are also still derived from that dream-like and "empty" state, and so contact with that realm is equally necessary in scientific thinking or in psychoanalytic practice, thinking, or writing.

The passion for truth

"Investigate the caesura", Bion (1977a) suggested, "not the analyst; not the analysand; not the unconscious; not the conscious; not sanity; not insanity. But the caesura, the link, the synapse" (p. 56). Meaning originates and exists in the interstices of these links, both inter-personal and intrapsychic; it is neither in the patient nor in the ana-lyst, neither in the mother nor the infant, but "in the bit in between". Being, or mindfulness, is to be found in those spaces where dreams and imagination mate with reason and gestate into thoughts, ideas, interpretations, poems, music, etc. In a sense, meaning is created where there is nothing yet to be found.

Mental health demands that we give shape and form to the dreams that reside in the emptiness, what Shakespeare described as the "airy nothing" of imagination which occupies our minds.

> Lovers and madmen have such seething brains,
> Such shaping fantasies, that apprehend
> More than cool reason ever comprehends . . .
> One sees more devils than vast hell can hold,
> That is the madman: the lover, all as frantic,
> The poet's eye, in a fine frenzy rolling,
> Doth glance from heaven to earth, from earth to heaven;
> And as imagination bodies forth
> The forms of things unknown, the poet's pen
> Turns them to shapes, and gives to airy nothing,
> A local habitation and a name.
>
> (Shakespeare, 1600, V(i): 4–14)

We *are* the "airy nothings" of our dreams, and our capacity to exist in that non-existent world enables us to feel we exist in this one, as "imagination bodies forth" from the unknown and otherwise unknowable realm into the world of phenomena, and the elusive thoughts, no matter how mad, which make us real.

One sometimes has to wonder what draws people to be engaged in the often disturbing and infinitely complex world of the mind. This poem by sixteenth-century poet–dramatist, George Chapman, describes the kind of spirit willing to withstand the mystery and uncertainty of these experiences.

> Give me a spirit that on this life's rough sea
> Loves to have his sail filled with a lusty wind
> Even till his sail-yards tremble, and his masts crack . . .
> There is no danger to a man that knows
> What life and death is . . .
>
> (Rolfe, 1883, p. 35)

To know life is to be a willing participant in the deaths of obsolete aspects of the self that deaden the mind. Both analyst and analysand face these issues of the life and death of the self, and both have to be willing to crack, to love the danger and insecurity of a mind based on impermanence but in the service of real, though fleeting, flashes of knowledge. Without this, one lacks a sense of security, one cannot rely on one's own mind, a crippling uncertainty which lies at the heart of all states of confusion. This obstacle to the development of thinking causes anxiety and depression, psychic retreats, and stymies action in obsessive–compulsive disorders. Shakespeare once again says it far better than anyone.

> And thus the native hue of resolution
> Is sicklied o'er with the pale cast of thought,
> And enterprises of great pitch and moment
> With this regard their currents turn awry,
> And lose the name of action.
>
> (1621, III(i): 84–88)

The need to know the truth at whatever cost is expressed in Nietzsche's (1882) famous axiom, "*Amor fati*", which describes this need to "love fate", to embrace one's destiny wherever it might lead.

> I want to learn more and more to see as beautiful what is necessary in things . . . Amor fati: let that be my love henceforth. I do not want to wage war against what is ugly. I do not want to accuse; I do not even want to accuse those who accuse . . . I want to be a Yes-sayer. (Nietzsche, 1882, p. 223, sec. 277)

Bion's willingness to question the essence of psychoanalytic work exemplifies his love of fate and his faith in the unknown destiny of embracing truth. The potential for destruction in analysis is a necessary aspect of the work, as the reign of the patient's false self is challenged and usurped. Such a patient finds himself "deconstructed", as one of my patients described it, a frightening experience of transition to an unknown destination. To accept one's fate is to recognise that in that loss and suffering, unknown aspects of the mind might arise to connect one to an authentic self.

"O" and the future of analysis

Nietzsche's idea that the *Übermensch* was a mental development which would have to wait for further evolution is echoed in Bion's

"Übermensch", for his higher man is the mystic, or exceptional individual. This is an exceedingly important and challenging idea, for it requires that we recognise this kind of mental development as still very much before its time. Not yet having developed the necessary mental conditions to facilitate this quantum mental leap, we might say that the missing link between man and ape is, in some ways, yet to evolve. The human race, that is, is yet to evolve into a real Homo sapiens sapiens—we are smart, but we are not sapient.

Since O is viewed by Bion as the necessary state in which to practise psychoanalysis, associating O with the domain of the "mystic", or "genius", or "exceptional individual" points to the idea of a need for further mental evolution if we are to fulfil the challenge of psychoanalysis. This revolutionary idea is sure to be unpopular with the group, for it is an undemocratic idea, requiring us to question our work, and implicit in which is the idea that all analysts are not created equal. As Bion (1970) made clear in his theories about the mystic and the group, these are sobering challenges, which could be seen as dangerous to the future of psychoanalysis. On the other hand, however, if tolerated, they might instead provide the impetus for the kind of rigorous thinking which leads to change and growth.

Bion's theory of the mystic, or genius, therefore also requires our recognition, "beyond wrongdoing and rightdoing", "beyond good and evil", and beyond the primitive unthinking superego, that the "good enough mother" is often not good enough to help the infant develop those aspects of his or her mind. It is not a negative judgement of the parents, but, rather, a statement about the time it takes to evolve into our human potential. The mother might physically tend to her infant with loving concern and the best of intentions, but if she cannot provide containment for primitive emotional life, the infant's capacity for truth, for thinking, and for the birth of an authentic self might be aborted. This constitutes an emotional trauma that activates in the child's mind a hatred of truth based on confusion and fear.

I have tried to show the role psychoanalysis can play in effecting these mental births on which the existence of a mind capable of being, passion, and creativity depends. However, in a psychological era dominated by psychopharmacological treatment and short term and cognitive therapies, analysis is popularly seen as costly, time consuming, and often ineffective. While it is indeed costly in time and money, opinions about its effectiveness depend largely upon how one defines effectiveness in the realm of the mind. In fact, it depends upon how one defines the mind itself. Of course, it cannot actually be defined, but it nonetheless presents a compelling and fundamental attraction with the lure of the Sirens, or a Muse which tempts men and women to its invisible mysteries. Our interest is propelled by an intuitive sense that from this mysterious unknown we derive the treasures of the mind—our capacities for wisdom, creativity, and beauty. The fact that this temptress might also lure one to madness accounts for the opposing force of suspicion and repulsion.

The charges against analysis, in particular the charge that it is ineffective, might, in part, be explained by these dangers, by our fear and limitations, and by the fact that it represents a goal that can never be attained. All we can do is get glimpses of the truth, but these are important attempts to satisfy our need for growth toward the fulfilment of an instinctual human need. À propos of this, Bion quotes Poincaré, who said, "Thought is only a flash between two long nights, but this flash is everything" (Bion, 1992, Foreword).

The expenditures in time and money are undoubtedly matched by the emotional cost of such a journey toward consciousness, but if one is drawn to the task, one, at some point, learns that it is not the attainment of a goal to which one is drawn, but the process of development of one's mind as a container for truth. One is drawn to it by a belief that there is value in having a mind, the belief in the value of being alive for no reason other than that one *is* alive. As Vonnegut (2005) much more humorously put it, "We are here on Earth to fart around. Don't let anybody tell you different" (p. 54). Only in the freedom of a self capable of play, of "farting around", can one stumble upon the road to O, which is always there waiting if we are available.

Since there is no final goal, the idea of perfectability needs to be reframed as the *development toward* knowledge and the acceptance of truth. We human beings are ever seeking ways out of our minds, and so a practice aiming at the complex, painful, and difficult endeavour of putting us in touch with our minds naturally has a limited appeal. Still, analysts have a bias that the truth is important, and this short poem by Marianne Moore describes a similar bias among poets.

Poetry
I, too, dislike it. There are things that are more important beyond
    all this fiddle.

Reading it, however, with a perfect contempt for it, one discovers in
it after all, a place for the genuine.

(Moore, 1921, p. 457)

Because of its challenging nature, poetry, like psychoanalysis,
seems destined to remain of concern to a relatively small minority. But
the fact that psychoanalysis continues to exist bears witness to the
idea that despite the emotional costs and the fears of the unknown,
there is an intense and innate yearning for the "genuine", the essential truths which are necessary for mental health.

The challenge Bion posed, to feel and think at this fundamental
level in an infinite mental space, is the source of genuine discomfort
and fear. His ideas about mankind's hatred of the mind and of
thoughts, and the refuge sought in mindlessness (above, p. 104), delin-
eate the obstacles to mental evolution and the enormous scope of the
challenge. Nonetheless, once awakened to the difficulties as well as
the gifts of having a mind capable of mental wholeness, truth, passion,
and creativity, one develops a sense of responsibility to oneself and to
others to fight against the entropy of mindlessness which might otherwise destroy these gifts.

REFERENCES

Asimov, I. (1966). *The Neutrino: Ghost Particle of the Atom*. New York: Avon Books.

Bair, D. (1978). *Samuel Beckett, A Biography*. New York, London: Harcourt, Brace, Jovanovich.

Barnhart, R. K. (1988). *The Barnhart Concise Dictionary of Etymology*. New York: Harper Resource.

Beardsley, A., & Gray, J. (1904). *Last Letters of Aubrey Beardsley*. London: Longman's, Green.

Beckett, S. (1952). *Waiting For Godot*. In: *I Can't Go On, I'll Go On*. New York: Grove Press, 1986.

Beckett, S. (1957). *Endgame: A Play by Samuel Beckett*. New York: Grove Press.

Beckett, S. (1961). *Happy Days*. In: *Samuel Beckett: The Complete Dramatic Works*. London: Faber and Faber, 1986.

Beckett, S. (1979). A piece of monologue. In: *Samuel Beckett: The Complete Dramatic Works* (pp. 423–429). London: Faber and Faber, 1986.

Bion, W. R. (1953). Notes on the theory of schizophrenia. In: *Second Thoughts* (pp. 23–35). New York: Jason Aronson, 1967.

Bion, W. R. (1959). Attacks on linking. In: *Second Thoughts* (pp. 93–109). New York: Jason Aronson, 1967.

Bion, W. R. (1962a). *Learning From Experience*. London: Basic Books.

Bion, W. R. (1962b). A theory of thinking. In: *Second Thoughts* (pp. 110–119). New York: Jason Aronson, 1967.

Bion, W. R. (1963). *Elements of Psychoanalysis*. London: Basic Books.

Bion, W. R. (1965). Transformations. In: *Seven Servants* (pp. 1–183). New York: Jason Aronson: Basic Books, 1977.

Bion, W. R. (1967). *Second Thoughts*. New York: Jason Aronson.

Bion, W. R. (1970). *Attention and Interpretation*. London: Tavistock.

Bion, W. R. (1974). *Bion's Brazilian Lectures I*. Rio de Janeiro: Imago Editora.

Bion, W. R. (1975). *Bion's Brazilian Lectures II*. Rio de Janeiro: Imago Editora.

Bion, W. R. (1977a). Caesura. In: *Two Papers: The Grid and The Caesura*. London: Karnac, 1989.

Bion, W. R. (1977b). Lecture. UCLA NPI, Los Angeles.

Bion, W. R. (1977c). Private conversation. Los Angeles.

Bion, W. R. (1977d). Private seminar. Los Angeles, Bion's home.

Bion, W. R. (1978). *Four Discussions with W. R. Bion*. Strath Tay, Perthshire: Clunie Press.

Bion, W. R. (1991). *A Memoir of the Future*. London: Karnac.

Bion, W. R. (1992) *Cogitations*. London: Karnac.

Bion, W. R. (1997). *Taming Wild Thoughts*. London: Karnac.

Blake, W. (1790). *The Marriage of Heaven and Hell*. In: *William Blake: The Complete Illuminated Books* (pp. 412–416). London: Thames & Hudson, 2000.

Bolle, K. (Trans.) (1979). *The Baghavadgita*. Los Angeles, CA: University of California Press.

Borgogno, F., & Merciai, S. A. (2000). *W. R. Bion: Between Past and Future*. London: Karnac.

Brown, N. O. (1960). *Apocalypse and/or Metamorphosis*. Berkeley, Los Angeles: University of California Press, 1991.

Buber, M. (1970). *I and Thou*. New York: Charles Scribner's Sons.

Camus, A. (1955). *The Myth of Sisyphus*. New York: Vintage Books.

Cocteau, J. (1993). Exhibit at Severin Wunderman Museum, Orange County, CA. Written on an untitled drawing.

Cohen, L. (1992). Anthem. *The Future*. Los Angeles, CA: Columbia Records.

Cohen, L. (2005). *I'm Your Man*. Documentary film by Lian Lunson, Lionsgate & Sundance Channel.

Condon, W. S., & Sander, L. W. (1974). Neonate movement is synchronized with adult speech: interactional participation and language acquisition. *Science*, January, 1974.

Cookson, W. (Ed.) (1975). *Ezra Pound: Selected Prose.* New York: New Directions.

Cummings, E. E. (1950). *95 Poems.* New York: Harcourt Brace & World.

De Kooning, W. (1988). *Collected Writings.* New York: Hanuman Books.

Des Pres, T. (1988). *Praises and Dispraises.* New York: Penguin.

Dickinson, E. (1959). *Selected Poems and Letters of Emily Dickinson.* New York: Anchor Doubleday Press.

Edelman, G. (2006). *Second Nature Brain Science and Human Knowledge.* New Haven, CT: Yale University Press.

Fairbairn, W. R. D. (1940). Schizoid factors in the personality. In: *Psychoanalytic Studies of the Personality.* Hove: Brunner-Routledge, 1994.

Fairbairn, W. R. D. (1944). Endopsychic structure considered in terms of object-relationships. In: *Psychoanalytic Studies of the Personality* (pp. 82–136). Hove: Brunner-Routledge, 1994.

Fairbairn, W. R. D. (1952). *An Object Relations Theory of the Personality.* New York: Basic Books.

Flam, J. D. (1973). *Matisse on Art.* New York: E. P. Dutton.

Freud, E. (Ed.) (1960). *Letters of Sigmund Freud, 1873–1939*, T. Stern & J. Stern (Trans.). New York: Basic Books.

Freud, S. (1893f). Charcot. *S.E., 3*: 9–23. London: Hogarth.

Freud, S. (with Breuer, J.) (1895d). *Studies on Hysteria. S.E., 2.* London: Hogarth.

Freud, S. (1900a). *The Interpretation of Dreams. S.E., 4–5.* London: Hogarth.

Freud, S. (1911b). Formulations on the two principles of mental functioning. *S.E., 12*: 215–226. London: Hogarth.

Freud, S. (1914d). On the history of the psycho-analytic movement. *S.E., 14*: 7–66. London: Hogarth.

Freud, S. (1920g). *Beyond the Pleasure Principle. S.E., 18*: 7–64. London: Hogarth.

Freud, S. (1923b). *The Ego and The Id. S.E., 19*: 3–66. London: Hogarth.

Freud, S. (1927c). *The Future of an Illusion. S.E., 21*: 3–56. London: Hogarth.

Freud, S. (1930a). *Civilization and its Discontents. S.E., 21*: 59–145. London: Hogarth.

Freud, S. (1933a). *New Introductory Lectures on Psycho-Analysis. S.E., 22.* London: Hogarth.

Frost, R. (1939). The figure a poem makes. In: J. C. Oates (Ed.), *The Best American Essays of the Century.* New York: Houghton Mifflin Company, 2000.

Gilot, F. (1990). *Matisse and Picasso: A Friendship in Art.* New York: Doubleday.

Greene, B. (2004). *The Fabric of the Cosmos: Space, Time, and the Texture of Reality*. New York: Vintage Books, Random House, 2005.

Groddeck, G. (1929). *The Unknown Self,* London: C. W. Daniel.

Grotstein, J. (2000). *Who Is The Dreamer Who Dreams The Dream?* Hillsdale, NJ: Analytic Press.

Grotstein, J. (2007). *A Beam of Intense Darkness: Wilfred Bion's Legacy to Psychoanalysis*. London: Karnac.

Grotstein, J. (2011). Private conversation. Los Angeles.

Hawking, S. W. (1988). *A Brief History of Time*. NewYork: Bantam Books.

Helminski, K. E. (1993). *Love Is A Stranger,* VT: Threshold Books.

Hinshelwood, R. D. (2010). Making sense: Bion's nomadic journey. Unpublished paper presented at PCC Bion Conference, Los Angeles.

James, G. W. (1917). *Arizona The Wonderland*. Boston, MA: Page.

Jean, M. (Ed.) (1974). *Jean Arp, Collected French Writings*. London: Calder & Boyars.

Jung, C. G. (1968). *Analytical Psychology, Its Theory and Practice*. New York: Vintage Books.

Kafka, F. (1937). *The Trial*. New York: Knopf [reprinted New York: Schocken Books, 1992].

Keats, J. (1817). Letter to George and Thomas Keats, December 21. *The Selected Poetry of Keats*. New York: Signet Classic, New American Library, 1966.

Keats, J. (1820). Ode on a Grecian Urn. In: *The Selected Poetry of Keats* (pp. 252–253). New York: Signet Classic, New American Library, 1966.

Klein, M. (1946). Notes on some schizoid mechanisms. In: *Envy and Gratitude and Other Works 1946–1963* (pp. 1–24). New York: Delacorte Press/Seymour Lawrence, 1975.

Lakoff, G., & Johnson, M. (2003). *Metaphors We Live By*. Chicago, IL: Chicago University Press.

Lebost, B. (2008). *The Universal Properties of Acceleration*. Indianapolis, IA: Author House.

Lebost, B. (2011). Private e-mail correspondence.

Leppman, W. (1984). *Rilke: A Life*. New York: Fromm International Publishing.

Mancia, M. (2006). Implicit memory and early unrepressed unconscious: their role in the therapeutic process (How neurosciences can contribute to psychoanalysis). *International Journal of Psychoanalysis, 87*(1): 83–103. Retrieved from PEP Archive database (IJP.087.0083A).

Mascaró, J. (Trans.) (1965). *The Upanishads*. London: Penguin.

Matisse, H. (1947). *Jazz*. Munich: Piper-Bucherei.

Matte-Blanco, I. (1975). *The Unconscious as Infinite Sets: An Essay In Bi-logic*. London: Duckworth.

McGuire, W., & Hull, R. F. C. (Eds). (1977). *C. G. Jung Speaking: Interviews and Encounters*. Bollingen Series XCVII. Princeton, CT: Princeton University Press.

Meltzer, D. (1981). Memorial meeting for Dr Wilfred Bion. *International Review of Psychoanalysis, 8*: 11–14 [republished as "The diameter of a circle" in the work of Wilfred Bion. In: D. Meltzer (Ed.), *Sincerity and Other Works* (pp. 469–474). London: Karnac, 2004].

Meltzer, D., & Williams, M. H. (1988). Aesthetic conflict: its place in development. In: *The Apprehension of Beauty*. London: Karnac, 2008.

Mettinger, T., & Cryer, F. (2005). *In Search of God: The Meaning and Message of the Everlasting Names*. Philadelphia, PA: Fortress Press.

Mitchell, S. (2009). *Sonnets to Orpheus*, Rainer Maria Rilke. New York: Vintage Books, Random House.

Moore, M. (1921). Poetry. In: *The Norton Anthology of Modern Poetry: Second Edition* (p. 457). New York: W. W. Norton, 1988.

Muller, J. P., & Richardson, W. J. (1982). *Lacan and Language: A Reader's Guide to Écrits*. New York: International Universities Press.

Neruda, P. (1974). *Neruda: The Book of Questions*. Port Townsend, WA: Copper Canyon Press.

Nietzsche, F. (1878). *Human, All Too Human: A Book for Free Spirits*. Cambridge: Cambridge University Press, 1986.

Nietzsche, F. (1882). *The Gay Science*. New York: Vintage Books, 1974.

Nietzsche, F. (1885a). *Thus Spoke Zarathustra*. London: Penguin Classics, 1961.

Nietzsche, F. (1885b). *Twilight of the Idols*. London: Penguin Classics, 1968.

Nietzsche, F. (1886). *Beyond Good and Evil*. New York: Random House, 1966.

Nietzsche, F. (1888). *Will To Power*. New York: Vintage Books, 1968.

Norman, J. (1999). Freedom to play, dream and think. *Scandinavian Psychoanalytical Review* 22: 172–188.

Norman, J. (2001). The psychoanalyst and the baby: a new look at work with infants. Presented at the James S. Grotstein Lectureship Conference. Los Angeles: UCLA, 3 February 2001.

Norman, J. (2004). Transformations of early infantile experiences: a 6-month-old in psychoanalysis. *International Journal of Psychoanalysis, 85*: 1103–1122.

Ogden, T. (1996). Reconsidering three aspects of psychoanalytic technique. *International Journal of Psychoanalysis, 77*: 883–899.

Pagels, E. (1989). *The Gnostic Gospels.* New York: Vintage Books.

Pally, R. (1997). Memory: brain systems that link past, present and future. *International Journal of Psychoanalysis, 78*: 1223–1234 [retrieved from PEP Archive Database (IJP .078.1223A)].

Paul, M. (1997). On the imitation of human speech. In: *Before We Were Young.* Birmingham, New York: Esf.

Peters, H. F. (1962). *My Sister, My Spouse: A Biography of Lou Andreas-Salomé.* New York: W. W. Norton.

Pistiner de Cortinas, L. (2009). *The Aesthetic Dimension of the Mind.* London: Karnac.

Plato (360 BC). Phaedo. In: *The Republic*, B. Jowett (Trans.) (pp. 81–153). Roslyn, New York: Walter J. Black, 1942.

Plato (380 BC). Ion. In: *The Collected Dialogues of Plato.* Bollingen Series LXXII. Princeton, NJ: Princeton University Press, 1961.

Pound, E. (1934). *A B C Of Reading.* New York: New Directions Paperbook, 1960.

Read, H. (1974). *A Concise History of Modern Painting.* London: Thames & Hudson.

Reiner, A. (1990). *Mind Your Head.* Los Angeles, CA: Wilshire House Press.

Reiner, A. (1994). *The Naked I.* Lancaster, CA: Red Dancefloor Press.

Reiner, A. (2002). *Beyond Rhyme & Reason.* Lancaster, CA: Red Dancefloor Press.

Reiner, A. (2009a). The aesthetic conflict as a function of early emotional trauma. Unpublished paper presented to the EBOR conference on Meltzer, Seattle.

Reiner, A. (2009b). *The Quest for Conscience and The Birth of the Mind.* London: Karnac.

Reiner, A. (2010a). Pre-verbal language in the treatment of a mother and infant: a clinical exploration. In: J. Van Buren & S. Alhanati (Eds.), *Primitive Mental States* (pp. 155–174). London: Routledge.

Reiner, A. (2010b). Unpublished poem.

Rhode, E. (1995). Does Mind have boundaries in the way that Body does? WMIP Jungian Public Lecture.

Rilke, R. M. (1902). *Letters To A Young Poet.* New York: W. W. Norton, 1934.

Rilke, R. M. (1912a). *Duino Elegies*, S. Mitchell (Trans.). New York: W. W. Norton, 1978.

Rilke, R. M. (1912b). *Duino Elegies*, D. Young (Trans.). New York: Vintage Books, 2001.

Rolfe, W. J. (Ed.) (1883). *Shakespeare's Sonnets*. New York: American Book Company.

Rosenfeld, H. (1978). *Impasse and Interpretation*. New York: Routledge.

Rubin, W. (Ed.) (1980). *Pablo Picasso: A Retrospective*. New York: The Museum of Modern Art.

Rumi (1984). *Open Secret*, J. Moyne & C. Barks (Trans.) Vermont, VA: Threshold Books.

Rumi (1993a). *Magnificent One*. N. O. Ergin (Trans.). New York: Larson.

Rumi (1993b). *Love Is A Stranger*, K. Helminski (Trans.). Vermont, VA: Threshold Books.

Rumi (1994). *Signs Of The Unseen: The Discourses of Jalaluddin Rumi*, W. M. Thackston (Trans.). Vermont, VA: Threshold Books.

Rumi (2003). *Rumi, The Book of Love*, C. Barks (Trans.). New York: Harper.

Scharff, D., & Birtles, E. (1994). *W. R. D. Fairbairn: Psychoanalytic Studies of the Personality*. Hove: Brunner-Routledge.

Schwartz, D. (1954). Coriolanus and his mother: the dream of one performance. Act three, 'There is a world elsewhere'. In: *Selected Poems: Summer Knowledge* (pp. 106–120). New York: New Directions, 1967.

Segal, H. (1981). Notes on symbol formation. In: *The Work of Hanna Segal: A Kleinian Approach to Clinical Practice* (pp. 49–68). New York: Jason Aronson.

Shakespeare, W. (1600). *A Midsummer Night's Dream*. In: *The Complete Illustrated Shakespeare*. New York: Park Lane, 1979.

Shakespeare, W. (1621). *Hamlet*. New York, Toronto: New American Library, Signet Classics.

Stein, G. (1913). Sacred Emily. In: *Geography and Plays*. Boston, MA: Four Seas, 1922.

Stein, G. (1935). What are masterpieces and why are there so few of them? In: J. C. Oates (Ed.), *The Best American Essays of the Century* (pp. 131–138). New York: Houghton Mifflin Company, 2000.

Symington, J., & Symington, N. (1996). *The Clinical Thinking of Wilfred Bion*. London: Routledge.

Symington, N. (1994). *Emotion and Spirit*. London: Karnac, 1998.

Tagore, R. (1913). *Gitanjali*. New York: Macmillan [reprinted New York: Scribner Poetry, 1997].

Thackston, W. M. (1994). *Signs of the Unseen: The Discourses of Jalauddin Rumi*. Vermont, VA: Threshold Books.

Trilling, L. (1950). *The Liberal Imagination: Essays on Literature and Society.* New York: New York Review of Books, 1978.

Valery, P. (1950). *Selected Writings of Paul Valery.* New York: New Directions.

Vonnegut, K. (2005). *A Man Without A Country.* New York: Random House Trade Paperbacks, 2007.

Walsh, J. (Trans.) (1981). *The Cloud of Unknowing.* Paulist Press Classics of Western Spirituality [reprinted New York: Harper Collins, 2004].

Welles, O., Bogdanovich, P., & Rosenbaum, J. (Eds.). (1998). *This Is Orson Welles.* New York: Da Capo Press.

Winnicott, D. W. (1971). *Playing & Reality.* London: Tavistock.

Yeats, W. B. (1997[1912]). Preface. In: R. Tagore, *Gitanjali* (pp. 7–42). New York: Scribner Poetry.

Young, J. (2005). *Schopenhauer.* New York: Routledge.

INDEX

Walsh, J., 62, 158
Welles, O., 145, 158
Williams, M. H., 121, 155
Winnicott, D. W., 19, 126, 143, 158
world
    aesthetic, 52
    analytic, xi, xiv
    emotional, 53
    ephemeral, 60
    external, 14, 20, 42, 69, 98
    infinite, 39
    internal, 14, 19, 25, 46, 51, 53, 63
    invariant, 5
    loveless, 28
    natural, 6

non-verbal, 33, 47
physical, 45, 55, 60
primitive, 27
psychic, 19
real, 28, 66
scientific, 4
sensual/sensuous, 3, 13, 21,
    145
variant, 5
visible, 5

Yeats, W. B., 23, 158
Young, J., 17, 22, 158

Zarathustra, 8, 133, 139

For Product Safety Concerns and Information please contact our EU
representative GPSR@taylorandfrancis.com
Taylor & Francis Verlag GmbH, Kaufingerstraße 24, 80331 München, Germany

www.ingramcontent.com/pod-product-compliance
Lightning Source LLC
Chambersburg PA
CBHW050513280326
41932CB00014B/2300